Bamboo Wood Ivory and Horn Carving

Highlights of Auctioned Chinese Antiques

WRITTEN BY : Xiao Yuan
TRANSLATED BY : Zhao Yahui, Yu Jiamin

CTS | Hunan Fine Arts Publishing House

图书在版编目（CIP）数据

竹木牙角雕 : 英文 / 晓原编著. — 长沙 : 湖南美术出版社, 2012.3（中国古董拍卖精华）

ISBN 978-7-5356-5217-1

Ⅰ.①竹. Ⅱ.①晓. Ⅲ.①竹刻－拍卖－中国－古代－图集②木雕－拍卖－中国－古代－图集③牙雕－拍卖－中国－古代－图集 Ⅳ.①F724.59-64

中国版本图书馆CIP数据核字(2012)第040242号

Bamboo, Wood, Ivory and Horn Carving of Highlights of Auctioned Chinese Antiques

PUBLISHER: LI XIAOSHAN

SUPERVISOR: ZHANG XIAO, YAN HUA

AUTHOR: XIAO YUAN

TRANSLATOR: ZHAO YAHUI, YU JIAMIN

EDITOR IN CHARGE: LIU HAIZHEN, LIU YINGZHENG

PROOF-READING: XU DUN

GRAPHIC DESIGN: XIAO RUIZI, HU SHANSHAN, SHU XIAOWEN

PLATE-MAKING: SUN YAN, XIONG JIE

ENGLISH EVALUATION: XIAO FANG

PUBLISHING AND DISTRIBUTION HOUSE: HUNAN FINE ARTS PUBLISHING HOUSE (NO.622, SECTION 1, EASTERN BELTWAY 2, CHANGSHA, HUNAN, CHINA)

DISTRIBUTOR: HUNAN XINHUA BOOKSTORE CO., LTD.

PRINTING HOUSE: SHENZHEN HUA XIN PRINTING CO., LTD.

SIZE: 787 × 1092 1/16

SHEETS: 10

VERSION: MAY 2012, FIRST EDITION;
          MAY 2012, FIRST PRINTING

ISBN: ISBN 978-7-5356-5217-1

PRICE: USD $19.90/ CNY ￥98.00

CONTENTS

II. Wood Carvings

III. Ivory Carvings

IV. Horn Carvings

Guide to the Use of This Series

1. "Highlights of Auctioned Chinese Antiques" comprises five volumes, namely, "Bamboo, Wood, Ivory and Horn Carvings", "Porcelain", "Jadeware", "Bronzeware" and "Ancient Furniture". Each volume contains around 150 representative items put up for auction from 1995 to 2010 at auctions held by dozens of auction companies from cities like New York, Nagel, London, Hong Kong, Macau, Taipei, Beijing, Shanghai, Tianjin, Nanjing, Guangzhou, Kunming, Chengdu and Jinan. The selection of the items is based on the style, texture, form, decorative pattern, workmanship, function, cultural implication and value of the antiques in question, including some items which have not yet been transacted.

2. Each volume retains the original record of auctions and the items are arranged in order of dynasty, name, dimension, transaction price (or estimate price), auction company, date of transaction and item analysis.

3. Due to different origins of auction companies, the prices of the antiques in US dollar, Euro, Great Britain Pound, Hong Kong dollar or Taiwan dollar, have been converted into RMB according to current exchange rates.

Preface

Market Survey of Bamboo, Wood, Ivory and Horn Carvings

XIAO YUAN

Bamboo, wood, ivory and horn carvings used to attract little attention over the years. However, small as they are, they are an important category in China's arts and crafts, noted for their rare materials, exquisite workmanship and long history. It is for this reason that they have begun to arouse the interest of collectors in recent years. Since 2003, in particular, they have become new favorites on the artwork investment market.

Ⅰ. Market Trend

1. From obscurity to popularity

Collectors used to focus on calligraphic works, paintings and porcelain, leading to the obscurity of bamboo, wood, ivory and horn carvings, which were transacted at very low prices. Beginning from 1993, the collection of bamboo, wood, ivory and horn carvings started to come to the fore and some items were transacted at the price of hundreds of thousands of Renminbi at a number of antique auctions. After a period of 10 years, due to skyrocketing porcelain prices in 2005, many collectors shifted their attention to bamboo, wood, ivory and horn carvings, resulting in their soaring prices.

1) Bamboo carvings

Bamboo carvings refer to bamboo wares carved with decorative patterns and/or inscriptions and ornaments carved out of bamboo root. Since the mid-Ming Dynasty, Jiading and Jinling, home to bamboo, became centers of bamboo carving and a large number of famous bamboo carvers were produced. The unique style of bamboo carvings has made them favorites of collectors since ancient times. Traditional carving techniques include openwork carving, bas-relief carving, circular carving, Fanhuang carving and Liuqing carving (Fanhuang carving refers to carving of bamboo arts and crafts after its green outer coating has been removed, and then it is boiled, dried and pressed flat, with its inside facing outwards. It is then polished and carved with patterns such as figures, landscapes or flowers and birds. Such handicrafts are generally in the form of fruit bowls and stationery receptacles. Liuqing carving means carving directly on the green outer coating of bamboo).

From 1994 to 2004, a great number of treasured bamboo carvings were transacted at very high prices at auctions by such auction companies as Sotheby's, Christie's and Guardian. In 2000, a bamboo carving entitled "Seven Gentlemen of the Bamboo Forest" dating back to the end of the Ming Dynasty and the beginning of the Qing Dynasty were auctioned at the price of RMB 423,500, twice the estimated price. In 2001, a brush holder with figure and building pattern dating back to mid-Qing Dynasty was sold at the price of RMB 4,160,000. In 2002, a 12-centimeter-high brush holder with Liuqing landscape and figure pattern dating back to the Reign of Emperor Kangxi of the Qing Dynasty was sold at a Christie's auction at the price of RMB 1,590,000. And from 2003 to 2005, a number of bamboo carvings were auctioned at the price of hundreds upon thousands of Renminbi.

2) Wood carvings

Wood carving refers to wooden decorative art or wooden wares with decorative patterns. Wood with tough and hard texture, such as nanmu, red sandalwood, boxwood, agalloch eaglewood, redwood, longan wood and camphor wood, are usually used as the raw materials, and carving techniques include circular carving, bas-relief carving and piercing, or with several techniques combined. Some are painted and colored to beautify and protect the wood. Root carvings refer to arts and crafts carved out of roots of trees according to their natural shapes, and the categories range from rosewood root and longan root carving to golden lacquer carving, Xiangnan carving and Huizhou carving. Since 1993, there has been an increasing interest in wood carving and prices have been rocketing on the auction and investment market.

In November 1998, a Sakyamuni statue wood carving dating back to the Reign of Emperor Yongle of the Ming Dynasty was transacted at a Christie's auction at the price of RMB 680,000. In 1999, a golden lacquer sitting Buddha was transacted at a Hanhai auction at the price of RMB 506,000. In 2000, a wood carving Buddha was transacted at a Sotheby's auction at the price of RMB 4,114,000.

Wood carving is a perfect combination of natural beauty and human workmanship, and a lot of wood carvings have been sold at high prices in the past decades.

3) Ivory carvings

Ivory carvings refer to carvings with ivory as the raw material. Ivory is smooth in texture, clear as jade, fine in grains and beautiful as precious stone. When carved into arts and crafts, it is full of artistic charm and is much treasured by collectors.

In spite of their high artistic value and exquisite workmanship, ivory carvings were not very popular before the 1990s. Later on, after the promulgation of international law for the protection of endangered species in 1998 and the ban of ivory trade by many countries, there has been a shortage of ivory and prices of ivory carvings have been soaring up.

In 1995, an ivory carving Goddess of Mercy was transacted at a Hanhai auction at the price of RMB 605,000. In 2000, an ivory vase with the pattern of Immortals Celebrating the Birthday of the Queen Mother of the West was transacted at Tianjin Emperor's Ferry Auction at the price of RMB 605,000. In 2004, a pair of seals with dragon knobs dating back to the Reign of Emperor Tongzhi of the Qing Dynasty were sold at Shanghai Xinren Auction at the price of RMB 484,000, ten times the estimated price. And in 2005, an ivory bush washer with patterns of flowers and fruits (symbolizing happiness and longevity), which was only 16.8 centimeters in length, was transacted at a Hanhai auction at the price of RMB 110,000.

4) Horn carvings

Horn carvings refer to exquisite arts and crafts carved out of horns of rhinoceros, cattle, sheep, roe deer or deer. Due to its high medicinal value, rhinoceros horns were as treasured as luminous wine cups and precious stones in ancient times. Today, rhinoceros is protected as an endangered animal and rhinoceros horn is no longer a raw material of carving, thus leading to its rarity and preciousness. And the prices of rhinoceros horn carvings are getting higher and higher with each passing day.

In 1995, a rhinoceros horn cup of the Ming Dynasty was sold at a Hanhai auction at the price of RMB 454,500. In 1996, a rhinoceros horn wine vessel with Zhou Tianqiu's inscription dating back to the Reign of Emperor Wanli of the Ming Dynasty was sold at a Hanhai auction at the price of RMB 220,000. In 2000, a rhinoceros horn wine vessel with animal and thunder pattern dating back to the Reign of Emperor Qianlong of the Qing Dynasty was transacted at a Christie's auction at the price of HKD 980,000. In 2001, a rhinoceros horn carved with Maitreya Buddha pattern was sold at a Hanhai auction at the price of

RMB 1,097,800. In 2004, a rhinoceros horn rockery with the pattern of the Eighteen Arhats dating back to the Ming Dynasty was transacted at the price of RMB 1,276,000. And there were numerous examples of rhinoceros horn carving transactions at high prices in auction markets.

2. From readjustment to a new height

From 2006 to 2008, bamboo, wood, ivory and horn carvings underwent a period of readjustment, and since 2009, the market has witnessed a boost and confidence in the market has been increasing.

1) Bamboo carvings

In 2006, in spite of the readjustment of the market, a number of bamboo carvings were transacted at considerably high prices. In 2009, the market was affected by the global financial crises, but the prices of articles with unique features were steadily on the rise.

2) Wood carvings

Prices of wood carvings have been rising steadily since 2006 and there have been lots of examples at various auctions held by Guardian, Hanhai, Chieftown, Christie's and Sotheby's auction companies.

3) Ivory carvings

In 2006 and 2007, the prices of some ivory carvings reached more than a million or several million. In recent two years, with the lifting of the ban on ivory trade, the ivory carving market gained further momentum. In 2008, China's import of ivory maintained and boosted its ivory carving industry, thus leading to a new enthusiasm for the collection of modern ivory carvings, hence the saying "Rather ivory and rhinoceros horn than porcelain and bronze wares". Prices of a number of exquisite ancient articles have been soaring up.

4) Horn carvings

In 2006, despite the market readjustment, a couple of arts and crafts were transacted at the price of several million, owing to the very limited number of supply. Beginning from 2007, prices kept rising, and in

2010, prices were skyrocketing, resulting in the sky-high prices of some auctioned articles.

II. Orientation of Value

1. Genuineness

The genuineness of an article is undoubtedly the essential factor influencing its value. Collectors of bamboo, wood, ivory and horn carvings, like those collecting other kinds of arts and crafts, must have the ability to differentiate genuine articles from false ones. Reproductions and fakes are generally made in the following ways:

1) Materials

Horns and teeth of other animals are passed off as rhinoceros horns and ivories, and other woods are passed off as precious woods such as nanmu and rosewood.

2) Time periods

New carvings are made to look ancient.

3) Shapes and patterns

There are carvings which are made out of sheer fabrication.

4) Piecing

Part of an article is genuine, while other parts are forged, and the genuine and forged parts are pieced together to look like a genuine article.

5) Inscriptions

The article is genuine itself, but inscription of famous people is added to make it more authentic and expensive.

6) Modification

An old article is modified in some way or others.

It is quite necessary for collectors to have a good understanding of the styles, features, ways of appraising arts and crafts and the market situation. If you are not sure about some expensive articles, you can consult experts in this field.

Owing to the limited space of this book, we will next let you know how to examine rhinoceros horn carvings as an example.

Rhinoceros horn carvings were popular towards the end of the Ming Dynasty and at the beginning of the Qing Dynasty, seldom seen in the mid and late Qing Dynasty. Due to the rarity of rhinoceros horn, this kind of horn carvings are now very expensive, especially those by famous masters. Therefore, collectors should pay close attention to the examination and determination of old and new rhinoceros horn carvings. The following are ways of evaluation.

1) Material
The quality and time periods of rhinoceros horn can be determined through examining its texture, grain, smell, length, cross section and depth of muzzle.

2) Workmanship
Firstly, examine whether the carving is simple or complicated in design. Secondly, look at the designs and patterns on the article. Thirdly, check the patterns on the inner wall of an article. Fourthly, pay attention to the bottom and muzzle of an article, and lastly, take a close look at the content of the patterns.

3) Color and luster
Rhinoceros horn carvings of different time periods and quality differ in color and luster, which can be taken as criteria for the determination of good and commonplace articles.

2. Rarity of materials
Another major factor influencing the prices of bamboo, wood, ivory and horn carvings is the rarity of

materials. As the saying goes, "Things are precious when they are rare." Rhinoceros and elephants are endangered animals under international laws of protection, rhinoceros horn and ivory trade is banned in many countries, and therefore, they are almost unavailable on the market. Furthermore, rhinoceros horn and ivory carvings tend to become worn and corroded over time. All these lead to a very limited number of articles, which accounts for the very high prices on the collection and investment market.

3. Artistic standard

The artistic standard of an article is also an important factor influencing the price of the article. Take bamboo carvings as an example. South China is abundant in bamboo, so the very high prices of bamboo carvings depend on their artistic value. The artistic appeal, content, carving, exquisiteness, style and cultural connotation of an article are criteria of the price and collection value.

The same is true of wood, ivory and horn carvings.

4. Inscription by famous people

An investigation of the auction market situation reveals that articles transacted at high prices are mostly those with inscriptions of famous people or collected items of the Qing Palace. So we can see that the fame of famous people is an important factor influencing the prices of carvings. Representative artists, symbolic articles and classical items constitute the inherent core value of art, and the originality and innovativeness demonstrated by these works play a key role in the understanding of art and judgment of value.

5. Source of arts and crafts

Still another factor influencing the prices of bamboo, wood, ivory and horn carvings is the source of articles. Fine and authentic articles, those once in the collection of widely recognized appraisers and collectors, or those with much media publicity become the center of attention and target of collectors as soon as they appear on the market, since there is no problem about their artistic value and value of collection and appreciation. There is no lack of examples in this aspect. Arts and crafts once in the collection of Qing Palace, especially those made exclusively for the imperial palace and those with the inscriptions of emperors are transacted at sky-high prices.

6. Market factors

Bamboo, wood, ivory and horn carvings are closely related to the market of arts and crafts as a whole. Their prices vary from place to place and are influenced by conditions of circulation. The packaging and marketing of auction companies are also important factors influencing the transaction of articles, and information about the market is equally essential.

The pricing of collections in China is usually dependent on the principles of price ratio, quality, price, rarity of articles and prevailing market prices. Therefore, collectors should not only constantly enhance their standard of appraisal and build their differentiation ability, but also have a good knowledge of the current market situation.

In addition, the quality and time periods of arts and crafts are also factors influencing the price of an article. Improper preservation results in poor quality, thus affecting the price. By time period, we do not mean "the older, the better". The best are those produced in the heyday of the Ming and Qing Dynasties.

Nowadays, it has become a trend and a vogue to be involved in art collection, which is now a symbol of artistic taste. A retrospect of the market conditions of recent years and a prospect of future trend of development have revealed that bamboo, wood, ivory and horn carvings will have a bright future and huge market potentials.

Ⅰ. Bamboo Carvings

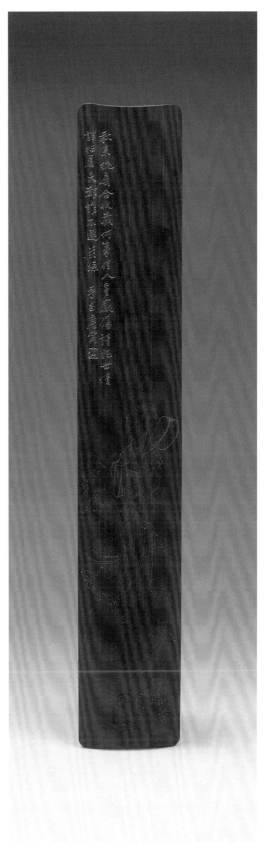

Carved Bamboo Armrest with Tang Yin's Painting of Chinese Traditional Beauty

Origin: Ming Dynasty
Length: 44.8 cm
Width: 7.6 cm
Hammer Price: RMB 253,000
Name of Auction Company: Sungari International
Date of Transaction: 2002-12-07

The carving on this bamboo armrest adopts line-drawing and light-engraving skills. The carver uses a knife instead of a brush to paint on the bamboo. The simple composition, fresh picture and vivid characters make it a rare work of art. The old collection with a silk sleeve having been preserved belonged to Yi Jin Zhai.

Tang Yin (1470-1523), better known by his courtesy name Tang Bohu, is a Chinese scholar, painter, calligrapher and poet of the Ming Dynasty. He is accomplished in poetry, prose and calligraphy, and excelled especially in painting. He is talented in painting landscape, human figures and flower-and-bird. Tang Yin is one of the painting elites"the Four Masters of Ming Dynasty"(Ming Si Jia), which also includes Shen Zhou (1427-1509), Wen Zhengming (1470-1559) and Qiu Ying (ca. 1501-1551). Tang Yin is also a talented poet. Together with his contemporaries Wen Zhengming (1470-1559), Zhu Yunming (1460-1526) and Xu Zhenqing (1479-1511), he has been known as one of the"Four Literary Masters of the Wuzhong Region". The lady with fan is a representative theme in his paintings.

Carved Bamboo Brush with Patterns of Bird and Flower

Origin: Reign of Emperor Wanli of Ming Dynasty (1573-1620)

Length: 23 cm

Hammer Price: RMB 990,000

Name of Auction Company: China Guardian

Date of Transaction: 2006-11-22

This bamboo brush consists of a barrel and a cap. It is shallow-carved with patterns of bird and flower around the whole body. With flourishing flowers and flying paradise flycatchers, a vivid image comes alive. There are regular script characters "Da Ming Wanli Nian Zhi" (made during the Wanli Reign of the Ming Dynasty) marked straightly at the end of the barrel. Though the brush is the smallest part in the "scholar' s four jewels", it is not easy to remain to the present day which makes it scarce and valuable.

With a dense and orderly layout of the decoration patterns on the barrel and its meticulous, accurate and clear carving, a simple and unsophisticated elegance has been demonstrated. The tip of this brush is soft and white. The beautiful design and craftsmanship make it a rarity with high artistic value.

Carved Bamboo Brush Pot Illustrating "Gui Qu Lai Ci" (Back Home Again) by Zhu Xiaosong

Origin: Ming Dynasty
Height: 14.6 cm
Hammer Price: RMB 1,100,000
Name of Auction Company: China Guardian
Date of Transaction: 2003-11-26

With an elegant and bright patina, this exquisite straight brush pot is a treasure of bamboo carving products from Ming Dynasty. High-relief carving technique was used to carve Tao Yuanming (a famous poet and hermit in Jin Dynasty, 365-427 AD) and an ancient pine tree with clustering leaves on the pot. The brush pot vividly illustrates a typical scene of Tao's leisure life in his seclusion. Liquor and chrysanthemum on the pot are also what Tao liked to describe in his poems. He was indifferent to fame and wealth and led a dignified life. The sentence engraved on it means "Made by Zhu Xiaosong in 1575".

Zhu Xiaosong was born in Shanghai and he was a master of bamboo carving in Ming Dynasty. His father Zhu Songlin and his son Zhu Sansong were also bamboo carving experts. The way of engraving in the pot is similar to that in another Zhu's bamboo product unearthed from a tomb in Shanghai in 1966, so this "Gui Qu Lai Ci" bamboo brush pot is sure to be an authentic work.

Bamboo-root Carving of Senior Monk by Zhu Sansong

Origin: Ming Dynasty

Height: 17.8 cm

Hammer Price: RMB 2,640,000

Name of Auction Company: China Guardian

Date of Transaction: 2003-11-26

This statue made of bamboo root is fine and elegant in its design. Sitting on the ground with a vestment holding in hands, the senior monk, in a plain cassock and straw sandals, is absorbed in sewing and mending. The old man, with a lined forehead, has a benign face lightened by a broad grin from ear to ear. Well proportioned and spaced, this work enjoys exquisite workmanship and unique ingenuity. It portrays a simple and honest senior monk whose state of mind can never be ruffled and, all we can feel from it is peace and harmony. The engraved regular script "Made by Sansong" in its base is the name of Zhu Sansong, an expert of bamboo-carving born in Jiading in Ming Dynasty whose birth and death year is unknown.

Carved Bamboo Brush Pot with Patterns of Musical Dance Scene

Origin: Ming Dynasty

Height: 16.6 cm

Hammer Price: RMB 132,000

Name of Auction Company: China Guardian

Date of Transaction: 2003-11-26

This brush pot is dark brown with an old and thick patina. The wall adopts bas-relief carving technique to display a vivid scene of musical dance. By using special carving techniques, it organically combines and blends scholars' leisure with poetic charms. The scholars' elegant taste can also be expressed precisely and vividly in this bamboo carved work. Besides, the composition, the knife-engraving technique and the carve style of ladies' hairstyle and costume of this pot are very similar to the one named carved bamboo brush pot Illustrating "peeking at a letter" by Zhu Sansong presently in the possession of the National Palace Museum in Taiwan. It was made by bamboo carver from Jiading in Ming Dynasty with damages.

Bamboo-root Carving of Buddha's Hand Citron-shaped Decoration

Origin: Late Ming and Early Qing Dynasties

Length: 11.3 cm

Hammer Price: RMB 924,000

Name of Auction Company: Beijing Chengxuan

Date of Transaction: 2006-11-24

With ingenious combination of the smooth part of the slender root and the rough part of the thick root, this Buddha's hand citron-shaped decoration is made according to the natural shape of the bamboo root. In order to enhance the reality, the carver subtly highlighted the pits on the root, and engraved the fruits, the stems and the leaves vividly by using multiple techniques such as circular carving, openwork carving and polishing, etc. From all these techniques, we can see the typical bamboo-carving style of Zhu family from Jiading.

With rough and thick skin of the fruit, Buddha's Hand citron, belonging to a variety of the genus of Rutaceae, has medicinal efficacy. The scholar would place it on tables for perfuming rooms. In China the Buddha's hand citron symbolizes happiness and long life, because its name, "fo-shou", has those meanings when written with other characters. Therefore, works of art shaped like Buddha's hand citron are very popular around the world.

Bamboo-root Carving of Crab-shaped Decoration

Origin: Late Ming and Early Qing Dynasties
Length: 8 cm
Hammer Price: RMB 582,400
Name of Auction Company: Beijing Poly
Date of Transaction: 2009-05-30

"Crab" was an interesting subject in paintings and craftworks during the Ming and Qing Dynasties. This decoration is carved in full relief. The carver picked a bamboo root with root hairs and made full use of the natural shape of the cicatrice to carve the crab's eyes, shell and its eight claws which interlock. Instead of the static beauty, the decoration has captured a vivid dynamic moment of a crab. The ingenious selection of material, the excellent engraving technique and the wonderful design all make it a completely natural thing without a sign of artifact.

Carved Bamboo Brush Pot with "Hermits Climbing Mountain" and Inscribed Poem "Shudao Nan" by Pu Zhongqian

Origin: Early Qing Dynasty
Height: 13 cm
Hammer Price: RMB 1,684,608
Name of Auction Company: Hong Kong Sotheby's
Date of Transaction: 2004-10-31

The wall of this straight brush pot adopts relief carving technique and piercingtechnique to display a scene of the hermits, who have no fear of hardships and dangers, climbing the mountain. In the design, there are floating clouds on the top of the mountain; the structure below is solid and full of changes. Pines and willows are standing above the giant rock of the mountainside. Hermits who wear bamboo hats are making their ways down the narrow mountain road. The one in front is holding his halter in his left hand, while his right hand is pointing straight forward with a stick. He looks back, seems to talk with the fellows behind. Cliffs and running water are seen at the bottom of the scene.

"Shudao Nan" is a representative poem of Li Bai, the famous poet in Tang Dynasty. The poem describes the roads in Sichuan province are too steepy to march on, as a metaphor to care about his friend's safety and imply the country's fate.

Pu Zhongqian(1582-?), is the bamboo carving founder of "Jinling School"which keeps pace with "Jiading School".

Carved Bamboo Brush Pot Illustrating "Reporting Victory at Dongshan"

Origin: Early Qing Dynasty

Height: 15.8 cm

Hammer Price: RMB 127,865

Name of Auction Company: Hong Kong Christie' s

Date of Transaction: 2004-11-01

With a natural and smooth patina, this brush pot has straight sides which adopt low and high relief carving techniques. In the design, there stands an ancient pine tree near the cliff. Xie An, the famous general, is playing chess with an old man, with a maid and a boy standing beside. There comes a soldier whipping the horse on the mountain road, lifting a flag to report a victory. This scene was based on the famous Battle of Fei River at the time of the Eastern Jin Dynasty (317-420). The carver adequately represented the general' s manner of easiness and calmness by choosing this picture instead of a war scene. Compositionally, although many objects are included in the design, they are well-arranged and the details are abundant.

Carved Bamboo Brush Pot Illustrating "Liu Hai Playing with the Golden Toad" by Wu Zhifan

Origin: Early Qing Dynasty
Height: 15.7 cm   Hammer Price: RMB 2,240,000
Name of Auction Company: China Guardian
Date of Transaction: 2010-05-16

With an amber brown color and a smooth patina, this brush pot adopts low relief carving technique. On the exterior, the design depicts Liu Hai, sitting on a broom, with hair disheveled, robe unfastened, legs crossed and ancient coins between his fingers, is laughing and playing with a three-legged golden toad. An inscription in running hand reads "the Day After Great Heat in 1688. Made by Zhifan", so it can be told that it is the authentic work of Wu Zhifan of the Kangxi Reign.

Wu Zhifan was the leader in the prosperous period of Jiading bamboo carving in Shunzhi Reign and Kangxi Reign. His works had been chosen as excellent tributes for the emperor. Emperor Qianlong once spoke highly of his superb skills by inscribing a poem and then made it carved on Zhifan's work.

Carved Bamboo Brush Pot Illustrating "Zi Qiao Fu Xi" by Wang Zhiyu

Origin: Early Qing Dynasty
Height: 14.9 cm
Hammer Price: RMB 242,000
Name of Auction Company: Beijing Hanhai
Date of Transaction: 2005-06-20

With a smooth patina, this straight brush pot uses low relief carving technique. The way of carving was exquisite and proficient. This picture is originated from the story of Wang Qiao in the Eastern Han Dynasty, while people now use it as a metaphor for the difficulties to be an officer. In the design, Ziqiao is sitting on the ground with a bare belly. He is smiling toward the sky, with his leg crossed, and feet bare with shoes in one hand. There is a flower basket beside him with lucid ganodermas and other stuffs inside.

Wang Zhiyu was the great master of Jiading bamboo carving in the Reign of Emperor Kangxi. He retired from the world in his middle age, thus it makes his works scarce and valuable.

Liuqing-style (Skin-leaving Method) Carved Bamboo Brush Pot with Patterns of Landscape and Figure Made by Zhang Xihuang

Origin: Reign of Emperor Kangxi of Qing Dynasty
Height: 12 cm
Hammer Price: RMB 1,594,346
Name of Auction Company: Hong Kong Christie' s
Date of Transaction: 2002-10-27

This brush pot, shaped in a cylinder, is far more than a work after ancient style. Following the artistic conception and penmanship of Yuan Dynasty, its decoration is an independent creation. By applying the skin-leaving method skillfully, first incising patterns on the bamboo surface and then removing unnecessary material, this piece of work of antique style, with its line sliding in a smooth way, outstands itself in both technique and its lingering charm.

Zhang Xihuang, whose real name is Zong Lüe, is from Jiaxing, Zhejiang Province and was the initiator of raised characters in skin-leaving method active in the late Ming and early Qing Dynasties. Zhang' s bamboo carving is famous for its exquisite workmanship. There are only a few of Zhang' s works handed down to now, and the Brush Pot with Patterns of landscape and Pavilion collected in the Boston Art Museum is one of his representative works.

Carved Bamboo Brush Pot with Patterns of Landscape and Figure and Inscribed Poem by Zhou Naishi (Namely Mo Shan)

Origin: Reign of Emperor Kangxi of Qing Dynasty
Height: 14.5 cm   Diameter: 11.4cm
Hammer Price: RMB 1,980,000
Name of Auction Company: Beijing Council
Date of Transaction: 2007-06-03

Carved out of a compact bamboo joint, this brush pot is cylindrical with flat edge, and the bottom is made of diaphragm. It has a thick wall and three small feet. In the design, the external layer adopts intaglio technique. One side of the brush pot is carved with a poem "Poetry for Dao Mountains", which adds radiance and beauty to pictures on the outer wall.

The bottom signature inscription can tell that it was made by Mo Shan in the autumn of 1685. Mo Shan, known as Zhou Naishi, specialized in painting and carving. Plantain and bamboo are his frequent carving objects. Most of his works are characterized by "resemblance with the true shape, close to the real charm, and being embedded with the most interests". The brush pots in the Reign of Emperor Kangxi are rare, let alone the works by celebrities.

High-relief Carving Bamboo Brush Pot with Patterns of Landscape and Figure and Inscriptions of "Gu Jue" and "Zongyu"

Origin: Reign of Emperor Kangxi of Qing Dynasty
Height: 17.2 cm
Hammer Price: RMB 11,405,600
Name of Auction Company: Hong Kong Christie's
Date of Transaction: 2005-05-30

This brush pot has flat edges, straight sides and rosewood fitted mouth and bottom whose diameters are the same. The exterior is carved with landscape motifs including mountains, rivers, clouds, rocks, cliffs, bridges, trees and figures. Carving techniques like high relief carving, piercing and circular carving were used to carve the whole picture in a meticulous way. The composition is well-arranged, the design is delicate and the layer is clear.

Gu Jue(1662-1735), or "Zongyu", from Jiading, Jiangsu Province, was active in the Reign of Emperor Kangxi. He carried on the spirit of predecessors in Ming Dynasty but created his own style on bamboo carving. His works enjoyed a great popularity among the collectors in the Reign of Emperor Qianlong. Collectors were willing to pay a lot of money to buy one even it was damaged by fire.

Bamboo Carved Fragrance Holder Illustrating "The Meeting of Scholars in the Orchid Pavilion" by Gu Jue

Origin: Early Qing Dynasty
Height: 25 cm
Hammer Price: RMB 5,040,000
Name of Auction Company: China Guardian
Date of Transaction: 2010-05-16

This fragrance holder has a thick wall and shining amber color. The patterns are meticulous and exquisite, even the lateral space is carefully engraved. So it's another masterpiece that Zongyu devoted himself into and completely followed his heart. The picture on the wall is designed from the event that Wang Xizhi, the great calligrapher in Eastern Jin Dynasty, held a meeting for scholars in the Orchid Pavilion in the ninth year of Yonghe (353). Even and straight characters "Zongyu" inscribed on the cliff is the standard inscription format of Gu Jue. This fragrance holder is the biggest and most exquisite one in his works. He carried on the essence of techniques of predecessors, but also created his own style to lead the way.

Bamboo Carved Brush Pot Illustrating "Seeing-off Scene" in Romance of the West Chamber

Origin: Reign of Emperor Kangxi of Qing Dynasty
Height: 17 cm
Hammer Price: RMB 5,469,600
Name of Auction Company: Hong Kong Sotheby's
Date of Transaction: 2005-10-23

The shape of this brush pot is tall and straight. This "Seeing-off Scene" on the wall of this pot was in relief. It is based on the story of Yuan drama Romance of the West Chamber. In this scene, Zhang Sheng must travel to the capital and pass the Imperial Examination, and his lover Cui Yingying is seeing him off. In the design, the figures are precise, and the facial expressions are life-like, which highlights the sad feelings to say goodbye. The scene is peaceful and remote. The artist applies various background patterns to differentiate spaces. We can tell that this is a work of Gu Jue from the inscriptive name "Gu Jue" and "Zongyu". As a high-quality work of Gu Jue, this brush pot displays a complex composition and meticulously executed details.

Bamboo-root Carving of Herb-picking Elder

Origin: Qing Dynasty (17th Century/18th Century)
Height: 13.5 cm
Hammer Price: RMB 1,179,200
Name of Auction Company: Hong Kong Christie's
Date of Transaction: 2009-05-27

Carved out of bamboo root, this decoration is made according to the natural shape, thin above and thick below. The smiling elderly herb-picking man has his hair high in a bun, with long beards long over the chest, slender but sturdy. He wears a wide robe with a hide around the waist and straw sandals on the feet. Leaning on the mountain rock, he is holding a lucid ganoderma in his left hand while his right hand is touching the rock. In a basket beside him, there are bamboo twigs, peaches and lucid ganodermas which altogether have the meaning of "wishing you longevity" in Chinese. The old man looks perfectly natural and vivid. All the details show that it is a rare and excellent work.

Bamboo Carving of Eight Immortals by Cai Shimin

Origin: Qing Dynasty (18th Century)
Height: 8 cm
Hammer Price: RMB 3,484,125
Name of Auction Company: Hong Kong Christie's
Date of Transaction: 2007-11-27

The bamboos are carved into the Eight Immortals of Taoism in Chinese mythology. They are Han Zhongli, Zhang Guolao, Han Xiangzi, Tieguai Li, Lü Dongbin, Cao Guojiu, Lan Caihe and He Xiangu. Each immortal is holding his or her own power tool that can give life or destroy evils. These ornaments are in right and symmetrical proportions, and the figures' expressions are quite vivid. Skillful use of the knife-carving skill makes the engraving lines perfectly.

Cai Shimin was a master hand of bamboo carving from Jiading in Jiangsu Province in the mid-Qing Dynasty. He created upon the basis of the Feng family, and innovated his own style. Carving figures with bamboo root in full relief is what he did best. When he died, he was only 49. His works handed down for generations are very rare, which makes this set of the Eight Immortals extremely valuable.

Carved Bamboo Brush Pot with Patterns of Figure and Pavilion by Qing Gui

Origin: Mid-Qing Dynasty

Diameter: 14.7 cm

Hammer Price: RMB 4,160,000

Name of Auction Company: Paris Tajan

Date of Transaction: 2001-06-15

    This brush pot has the typical features of the multilayer-pierced bamboo carving. By combining the carving skill with the picturesque charm, the carver used the "level distance" viewpoint to unfold the full scenery. Although many people, houses and trees are included in the design, they are well-arranged. It shows how peaceful and happy the place is. In the auction market, it's the first piece of bamboo carving work after the Reign of Emperor Qianlong that the hammer price exceeds one million yuan.

    Qing Gui (1735-1816), whose first name is Zhangjia, was an official in Qing Dynasty. He died in 81 years old.

Carved Bamboo Brush Pot Illustrating Bamboo Carving of "Eight Horses"

Origin: Mid-Qing Dynasty
Height: 15.8 cm
Hammer Price: RMB 418,000
Name of Auction Company: Beijing Hanhai
Date of Transaction: 1995-04-12

   With a bright and smooth patina, this brush pot has straight sides which adopts multilayer piercing technique. The dynamic scene is well-arranged in composition. In the design, there is running water, vigorous trees and rugged rocks. With different postures, some horses are standing, some are lying, and the rest are leaning close to each other. Beside the stream, two horse-keepers in their official robes are relaxing under the tree. The painting"Eight horses"has been very popular since the Six Dynasties. In that picture, it draws eight fine horses which pulled the wagon for King Mu of Zhou in Kunlun Mountains. It also has the meaning of a galaxy of talents, and infers a Chinese old saying that the horse arrives, so does the success. This kind of theme is very common in bamboo carvings in the late Ming Dynasty.

Carved Bamboo Brush Pot Illustrating "The Meeting of Scholars in the Orchid Pavilion" by "Jing Feng Hermit"

Origin: Mid-Qing Dynasty
Height: 15.2 cm
Hammer Price: RMB 330,000
Name of Auction Company: Beijing Hanhai
Date of Transaction: 2002-07-01

This brush pot, shaped in a cylinder, adopts low relief carving technique around the whole body. It vividly records the picture that 41 scholars in Eastern Jin Dynasty including Wang Xizhi, Xie An and Sun Chuo gathered in the Orchid Pavilion to drink wine, wrote poems and played stringed instruments in the ninth year of Yonghe (353). The composition is well-arranged. It inscribed a full text of Orchid Pavilion Preface, the work of the great calligrapher Wang Xizhi, on the other side. It has 28 lines and 324 words. The Preface presents the highest state of Wang's calligraphy.

The engraving of Jing Feng Hermit retained the lingering charm of Wang's calligraphy. His carving techniques, artistic style of the theme and the composition show that he is from the school of Jiading bamboo carving. The "Hermit" culture got popular in the Early Qing Dynasty and it had extended to the Reign of Emperor Qianlong, thus Mr. Wang Shixiang once speculated that this kind of low relief brush pot should be made in the Reign of Emperor Qianlong.

Carved Bamboo Brush Pot with Patterns of Landscape and Figure by "Qing Xi Hermit"

Origin: Mid-Qing Dynasty
Height: 12 cm
Hammer Price: RMB 132,000
Name of Auction Company: Beijing Hanhai
Date of Transaction: 2002-07-01

The carver created a meticulous painting of landscape and figure on the brush pot. On the wall, it shows us mountains, pine trees, stream and weeping willows. Hermits are either talking or paddling a boat. The whole picture is fresh and elegant. The refined knife-carving skill, the accurate scale and the well-arranged composition make it a fine work in the mid-Qing Dynasty. It' s hard to find out who is Qing Xi Hermit, for lacking of information. But Mr. Wang Shixiang speculated that he may be a prolific bamboo carver with limited skill. Many imitations made by him are existed in the market.

Carved Bamboo Gui

Origin: Mid-Qing Dynasty
Height: 12.3 cm
Hammer Price: RMB 121,000
Name of Auction Company: Beijing Hanhai
Date of Transaction: 1995-04-12

A gui is a food container for holding glutinous millet, rice and sorghum, similar to the large bowl of today. It imitates the shape of the ancient bronze gui in Shang and Zhou Dynasties. The round vessel has a big mouth, a deep belly, two animal-head handles and a high foot ring. The upper part of the vessel is decorated with taotie (a Chinese ancient gluttonous ogre) patterns, and the body, with diamond lattice patterns and a raised pearl in the center of each lattice. On the foot ring are embossed taotie patterns. With the multilayer relief carving technique and the natural shape, this Gui vessel is an excellent imitation.

Carved Bamboo Square Box with Patterns of Pine, Bamboo and Plum

Origin: Mid-Qing Dynasty

Height: 5 cm

Hammer Price: RMB 132,000

Name of Auction Company: Beijing Hanhai

Date of Transaction: 1997-12-20

This oblong box is decorated with bamboo veneers. Stylized qiequ patterns frame the lid of the box. A dark pattern of the characters "shuangxi" is carved in relief to mean joy and auspiciousness. All sides are covered with dark bamboo veneers with patterns in relief. They are pines, bamboos, plums and orchids separately. This box is a rare artwork.

Carved Bamboo with Decoration of "Liu Hai Playing with the Golden Toad"

Origin: Mid-Qing Dynasty
Height: 24 cm
Hammer Price: RMB 330,000
Name of Auction Company:
Beijing Hanhai
Date of Transaction: 1995-10-07

The bamboo root that was used to make this decoration is plump and thick. The precise way of cutting and the excellent use of lines have represented the highest bamboo carving level of full relief in Qing Dynasty. The figures are vivid and the composition is well-arranged. In the design, Liu Hai is standing on the top of the hill and the toad is deep down in the valley, which exactly highlights high spirit of Liu and dullness of the toad. Liu Hai, in full relief, lying on the ground with his feet bare, is making fun of the toad. This whole decoration conveys a sense of joy, and perfectly performs the Taoist story of Liu Hai playing with the golden toad in folk legends. The toad in the story is a three-legged toad which can disgorge money. So the ancient people thought that the man who had it would be rich and happy.

Imperial Bamboo Carving Ruyi with an Inscribed Qianlong's Poem by "Gu Xiang"

Origin: Reign of Emperor Qianlong of Qing Dynasty

Length: 35 cm

Hammer Price: RMB 5,600,000

Name of Auction Company: Beijing Poly

Date of Transaction: 2010-12-06

Zhuhuang, also known as Wenzhu, Tiehuang, or Fanhuang, originating from the early Qing Dynasty and flourishing in the Reign of Emperor Qianlong and the Reign of Emperor Jiaqing, is an independent art form in bamboo carving. Zhuhuang, as the inner veneer of the bamboo, is light yellow. Its fresh and lovely luster is similar to the ivory. Fresh Zhuhuang veneer is taken from the large mao bamboo, and then through several procedures, it will be perfectly pasted onto an item no matter what the shape is. The junction would never be found.

Ruyi is an S-shaped ornamental scepter with a head in the shape of a glossy ganoderma or a cloud, and a slightly curved stem. In the center of the head, it is engraved with a pattern of the character "Shou", which means "longevity". Bat patterns are on the both sides of the character and also on the curved stem, as the word "bat" has the same pronunciation as the word "fortune" in Chinese. A poem made by Emperor Qianlong is inscribed at the back of the head with an inscription of "Gu Xiang". This simple and natural item reflects the special beauty of artistic bamboo items.

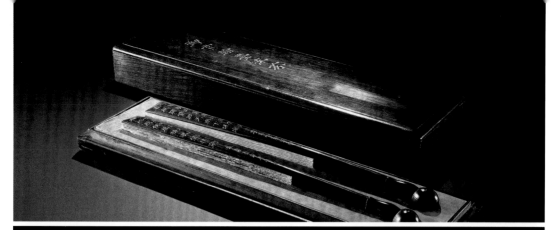

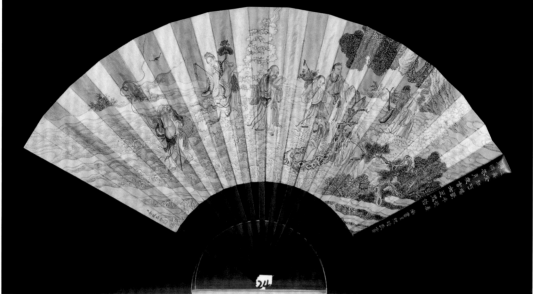

Imperial Folding Fans with a Fan Box (one set)

Origin: Reign of Emperor Qianlong of Qing Dynasty

Length: 38 cm   Hammer Price: RMB 672,000

Name of Auction Company: Beijing Poly

Date of Transaction: 2008-05-30

These folding fans each has 14 bamboo ribs. The joint of fan ribs are carved like "the monk's head". On the outside of the ribs, there are five-character quatrains carved respectively in intaglio with gold dust filled in. The artist's note "written by Jin Deying" is inscribed below the poem. Jin Deying(1701-1762), born in Renhe (now Hangzhou), Zhejiang Province, was the Number One Scholar in the first year of the Reign of Emperor Qianlong and then was granted the Xiuzhuan in Imperial Hanlin Academy. There is also an inscription engraved "written by Ji Yun" on the other fan. And the painting on the fan face is "the Eight Immortals Crossing the Sea". Ji Yun(1724-1805), also known as Ji Xiaolan, is the chief editor of Siku Quanshu (the Complete Library in Four Branches). He was a well-respected scholar and master in Qing Dynasty.

The two fans have a rosewood box to fit in perfectly. There is an ingenious design that two round holes cut through the bottom under the fan heads can help take the fans out easily. Popular in the period of late Ming and Early Qing, Fan with 14 ribs is relatively rare now. It's from the Royal Palace according to the contents and the exterior packing.

Carved Bamboo Oblong Boxes with Patterns of Dragons and Inscribed Imperial Poem

Origin: Reign of Emperor Qianlong of Qing Dynasty
Dimension: 34.3cm×18cm×11.6cm
Hammer Price: RMB 9,856,000
Name of Auction Company: Beijing Hanhai
Date of Transaction: 2009-11-11

Tiehuang products are much liked and admired by the royal. Ji Xiaolan even wrote poems to heap praise upon it. These two Tiehuang boxes mainly applied the traditional low relief carving technique and the gold inlaid technique in lacquer wares. Two erected dragons fighting in the sea of clouds are carved on the surface. Four emperors' poems with five characters to a line are respectively engraved on the interior surface of the lids. There is a drawer inside each box, and two paintings of landscape and figure by Dong Bangda are highlighted by the gold inlaid technique. An inscription of "drawn by Dong Bangda" is at the left bottom of each painting.

Dong Bangda (1699-1769), born in Fuyang County, was an officer and also a painter. As a painter, he is best at drawing landscape.

Carved Bamboo Brush Pot with Patterns of Landscape and Inscription of "Xingyouheng Tang"

Origin: Reign of Emperor Qianlong of Qing Dynasty
Height: 10.9 cm
Hammer Price: RMB 220,000
Name of Auction Company: Beijing Hanhai
Date of Transaction: 2004-11-22

This round brush pot has straight sides, an ivory fitted mouth and a same bottom. The landscape in low relief on the outer wall presents a quiet and peaceful scene in the mountain. The whole picture is filled with poetic beauty. "Xingyouheng Tang" was the exclusive clan title of the Prince Zai Quan(1794-1854) in Qing Dynasty. Zai was fond of collection, and he had also written the book "Collection of Xingyouheng Tang".

Carved Bamboo Brush Pot Illustrating "Boating with Cranes" by Wang Meilin

Origin: The Sixth Year of the Reign of Emperor Jiaqing of Qing Dynasty

Diameter: 12.7 cm   Height: 14.5 cm

Hammer Price: RMB 550,000

Name of Auction Company: China Guardian

Date of Transaction: 2006-06-03

This round brush pot has straight sides, a natural bamboo joint bottom, and three small feet. The curved mouth rim has inclined a little from outside to inside. It has a dark thick wall with a mild patina. The knife-carving skill is vigorous and firm. The design takes its story from Lin Hejing, the Gushan recluse of Hangzhou in Song Dynasty, boating on the river with his "sons"—cranes. There are an inscription of a poem dedicated to the story and the artist's inscription "made by Yungu in the spring of 1801". The wild but elegant patterns with highly artistically superb workmanship and exquisite modeling make this article a representative work in the early life of Wang Meilin, who was a mainstay of bamboo-carving art of Jiading school in the mid-Qing Dynasty.

Carved Bamboo Brush Pot with Patterns of "Five Elders" by Zhu Wenyou

Origin: Qing Dynasty
Height: 11.5 cm
Hammer Price: RMB 165,000
Name of Auction Company: Sungari International
Date of Transaction: 2004-06-07

This straight brush pot has a bright patina and it has been well-preserved. The wall adopts piercing technique to display a steep mountain and vivid figure expressions. The walking celebrities and the natural scenery, such as steep rocks, vigorous ancient pines, clouds on the sky, set each other off beautifully. By expressing the whole scene with only a small part, the picture tends to be neat, exquisite and clear. According to an ancient book"Popular Report in the Southern Song Dynasty", it is said that the"Five Elders"are five retired important officials who gathered together to enjoy wine and poetry in 1048. Because of the possession of integrity, ability and longevity, the"Five Elders" were heavily favored by literati through the ages. It has already become the symbol of "disgorge and happiness". Zhu Wenyou, born in Jiading in Qing Dynasty, was the son-in-law of Wu Zhifan.

Bamboo-root Carving of "He-He Er Xian"

Origin: Qing Dynasty
Height: 29 cm
Hammer Price: RMB 275,000
Name of Auction Company: Shanghai Jinghua
Date of Transaction: 2003-08-24

This decoration is made according to the natural shape of the bamboo root. By taking advantage of the entangled canes, the artist carved a lively He-He Er Xian statue with circular carving and piercing techniques. With pleasant and contented expressions on their round faces, the one of the immortals is standing on the mountain rock with lotus in hand, while the other one is squatting beside the former with money in hand and back against wisteria. A three-legged golden toad lying beside the rock is looking up to the two immortals. Its appearance balances the whole picture and adds some good fortune. He-He Er Xian also known as the "Immortals of Harmony and Union" or "the two spirits of Harmony and Union" are two Taoist immortals. They are popularly associated with a happy marriage. He and He are typically depicted as boys holding a lotus flower and a box. The exquisite workmanship and the unity of form and spirit make it a rare work of art.

Bamboo-root Carving of Seated Figure

Origin: Qing Dynasty

Height: 19 cm

Hammer Price: RMB 176,000

Name of Auction Company: Beijing Hanhai

Date of Transaction: 2000-07-03

This seated figure imitates the shape of Lohan. The artist strategically used the natural form of the bamboo root, and carved the lower thick part as a rock, the upper thin part as the figure sitting on the rock. With the eyes squinting and nostrils flaring, he is grinning happily. He puts his left hand on his right leg with a round cap in hand. Lifting his right hand, he seems to wipe his face with a cloth. And he raises his right leg on his erected left knee. With robe slid down, he reveals his plump arm muscle. On his feet, there is a pair of straw shoes with distinct texture. The skillful way of cutting makes the lines mellow and the expression delicate. It has a sense of grand and magnificent that the figure seems to seat on the top of the mountain.

Carved Bamboo Cup with Patterns of "Eight Immortals Drinking Merrily"

Origin: Qing Dynasty

Height: 8.5 cm

Hammer Price: RMB 220,000

Name of Auction Company: Beijing Hanhai

Date of Transaction: 2005-07-17

This cup has a wide flared mouth and a contracted belly. The scene of the Eight Immortals drinking freely with great joviality is carved on the exterior wall in high relief. In the design, the rocks stand in great numbers, and giant ancient pines are twisted with branches resembling a big umbrella. Under the tree, eight immortals are sitting around the table drinking. Various expressions and postures of the figures compose a lifelike image and highlight the broad-minded and bold character traits. The subject is based on the allusion of eight literati in the poem "Eight Immortals Drinking Merrily" (Yinzhong baxian ge) written by Du Fu, a great poet in Tang Dynasty. Its composition references a hand scroll painted by the famous artist Zhang Wo in the Yuan Dynasty.

Bamboo Veneer Ruyi with Patterns of "Three Abundances"

Origin: Qing Dynasty
Length: 36.5 cm
Hammer Price: RMB 110,000
Name of Auction Company: Beijing Hanhai
Date of Transaction: 1998-08-03

This ruyi is first covered with yellow bamboo veneers, and then with dark yellow veneers with various patterns in low relief. In the center of the head, it is decorated with peach patterns with twining branch patterns around. The curved shaft is veneered with finger citrons pattern in the middle and carved with a plum pattern and a pine pattern in low relief on its upper and lower parts respectively. The end has a lobed panel enclosing pomegranates. This combination of a peach, a Buddha's hand fruit and a pomegranate wishes to evoke longevity, fortune and fertility. The perfect unity of the wood and the veneer, the classic modeling and the superb workmanship make it an extremely excellent artwork of Tiehuang.

Carved Bamboo Armrest with Pine and Pavilion Patterns

Origin: Qing Dynasty
Length: 28 cm
Width: 7 cm
Hammer Price: RMB 200,000
Name of Auction Company: Duo Yun Xuan
Date of Transaction: 2002-12-09

On the front of this armrest, it is carved with vigorous pines, a silent valley and pavilions beside the stream. It seems that the sound of the running water can be heard. There is a poem engraved on the back with the artist's inscription of "Taoist Zhi". As famous as Wu Zhifan, the artist Zhou Hao(1685-1773) , born in Jiading, had other names as Zhou Zhiyan, Taoist Zhi and so on. He created a carving technique which is using knife to carve patterns directly on the bamboo. There is not so variable a thing in nature as his ways of cutting. He is considered as the first man who initiated a new bamboo carving technique in Qing Dynasty.

Liuqing-style Carved Bamboo Armrest with Willow and Myna Patterns

Origin: 1992
Length: 34 cm
Hammer Price: RMB 170,500
Name of Auction Company: Shanghai Xinren
Date of Transaction: 2004-12-08

This painting carved on the armrest belongs to Mr.Jiang Hanting, an old friend of Mr.Xu Subai. By using liuqing carving technique, the remaining bamboo skin is ivory white and it's decorative. In the design, the willow branches are swinging in the wind. There are two mynas singing on a branch, while another is flying away. The picture is lively and vivid with intense cultural atmosphere. Xu Bingfang, who is the son of the master of art Mr.Xu Subai, is a famous bamboo carving artist. He is hailed as the first liuqing artist in China. Moreover, Mr.Wang Shixiang considered him as the best modern bamboo carving artist.

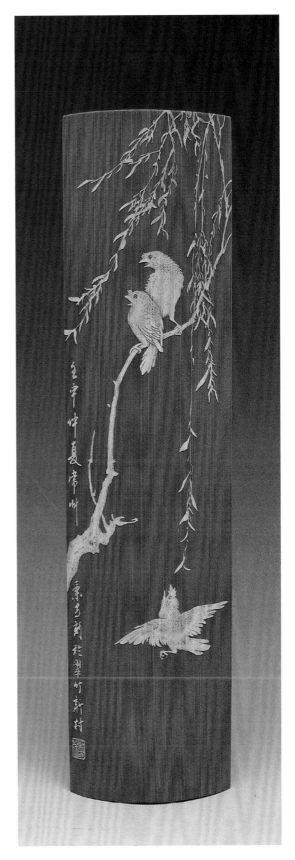

II. Wood Carvings

Painted Carved Wood Figures (one pair)

Origin: Eastern Zhou Dynasty
Height: 57.2 cm
Hammer Price: RMB 566,500
Name of Auction Company: Christie' s
Date of Transaction: 2000-03-22

This pair of figures is made of wood. The outline of the human body and the clothes were carved first and then the craftsman painted the eyes and brows with ink, lips with red color, and the clothes with red and black. One' s arms are slightly bent with hands clenched, and the other one hides his hands in the sleeves. The figures are tall and slim, and their expressions are serious and respectful. The remarkable thing is that two figures are still in good condition.

Painted Wood Figure of Warrior

Origin: Western Han Dynasty
Height: 43 cm
Hammer Price: RMB 487,600
Name of Auction Company: Chongyuan International
Date of Transaction: 2006-05-02

This warrior has a round face, broad eyebrows, long eyes, a high nose and a closed mouth. The figure is solemn and dignified. There is a scarf (a headwear for male in ancient China) on his head. Two pieces of cloth are pulled along his cheeks and tied beneath his jaw. He wears a black armour with red fish scales painted on it. A leather belt girdles around his waist. He is in high-top boots and the decorative patterns on it are also painted red. The warrior raises his right arm pointing the front with his left arm stretching downward. The face and the body are painted with red lacquer while the clothes with black. It is similar to the painted pottery warrior excavated in Shaanxi. According to the ranks of the painted pottery warriors in Shaanxi, this wood warrior is believed to be the highest commander of infantry warriors.

Carved Wood Figure of Bodhisattva

Origin: Song Dynasty
Height: 116.8 cm
Hammer Price: RMB 4,114,000
Name of Auction Company: Sotheby's
Date of Transaction: 2000-03-02

This Bodhisattva wears her hair in a high chignon. The posture is dignified and the expression is peaceful. The elements of realism increased in statue because of the popularity of idealist philosophy in Song Dynasty. This one has a sturdy body and broad shoulders with nothing on the waist. Gorgeous clothing makes her look like a noblewoman. She is sitting with her legs crossed. This vivid statue demonstrates extraordinary workmanship. It is extremely precious with its perfect condition.

Painted Carved Wood Figure of Water-moon Guanyin

Origin: Song Dynasty
Height: 156 cm
Hammer Price: RMB 8,938,040
Name of Auction Company: Hong Kong Christie' s
Date of Transaction: 2010-05-31

This statue made of wood is painted all over the body. The Water-moon Guanyin has a plump face, with the eyes nearly closed, and wears a high topknot. She seems in meditation with her eyes looking down. It is a typical female body but remains some masculinity. The upper part of the body is naked, with pearl and jade necklaces in front of the bosom. The arms are decorated with armlets. The Water-moon Guanyin, one of the 33 incarnations of Guanyin, is the product of Buddhism and Chinese native culture. The figure generally sits on the rock or the lotus throne. The Guanyin seems to enjoy the sight of the moon in the water in this position. The worship of Water-moon Guanyin had been very popular in the Song and Yuan Dynasties, and its effect was still visible till the Ming and Qing Dynasties.

Painted Carved Wood Figure of Guanyin

Origin: Liao Dynasty
Height: 107 cm
Hammer Price: RMB 176,000
Name of Auction Company: China Guardian
Date of Transaction: 2005-05-15

This Guanyin has a slender body and wears a high topknot with a crown on the top of the head. She has a mellow and full face, a high and straight nose, a closed mouth, long eyebrows and big ears. The expression is peaceful and heavenly. The upper part of the body is naked with a chaplet around her neck, bracelets on her wrists, and a shawl around her shoulder and arms. The Guanyin is dressed in a skirt with jewelries on it. With a horsetail whisk in the right arm and a pure vase in the left hand, she is standing on the lotus throne with bare feet. The statue is an exquisite work of art. The painting with lacquer was faded with age, and some clothes and ornaments have been repaired.

Painted Carved Wood Figure of Guanyin

Origin: Yuan Dynasty

Height: 110 cm

Hammer Price: RMB 896,000

Name of Auction Company: Chieftown Auction

Date of Transaction: 2007-11-04

This Guanyin is assembled by several pieces of wood with red, yellow, blue and green painted on the body. She has a high topknot, a plump face, a broad forehead with the eyes nearly closed. The expression is peaceful and heavenly. Wearing a long dress, the Guanyin is naked above the waist but with a mantle and jewelries. She is sitting on the angry lion. This Guanyin is called Bodhisattva Abhetri, one of the thirty-three forms of Guanyin. She is the symbol of fearlessness. Since Guanyin was introduced into China from India, and after a long-term intergration with Chinese culture, the worship to her has endured for centuries and she has become one of the most popular gods in China. The solemn but amiable sense of the Guanyin makes it a superior and excellent work.

Carved Wood Figure of Sitting Buddha in Golden Lacquer

Origin: Early Ming Dynasty

Height: 81 cm   Hammer Price: RMB 506,000

Name of Auction Company: Beijing Hanhai

Date of Transaction: 1999-07-05

With a topknot on his head, the statue has a high forehead and a high and straight nose. He looks dignified with eyebrows extending to temples and eyelids drooping. Behind him, the halo is like a flame. The Buddha in a plain kasaya is sitting cross-legged on a lotus throne, which embodies rebirth. Enjoying the traits of Buddha statues in Han Dynasty, the statue is a combination of openwork carving, circular carving and multilayer relief carving techniques. These three carving techniques bring out the best in each other without losing their respective features, making the statue an excellent work of mix and match. As for its artistic effect, it is resplendent and magnificent. Originated from Chaozhou, Guangdong Province, wood carving in golden lacquer is also called Chaozhou wood carving.

Carved Zitan (Padauk) Standing Figure of Sakyamuni Buddha

Origin: Reign of Emperor Yongle of Ming Dynasty
Height: 33.2 cm   Hammer Price: RMB 727,600
Name of Auction Company: Hong Kong Christie's
Date of Transaction: 1998-11-03

    This statue is carved out of zitan in full relief. Wearing a high coiled topknot, the Buddha has a round face, big ears, broad shoulders, and a strapping body. With eyes looking down, the statue exudes a sense of kindness. One-shouldered kasaya used the original color of the zitan with only carved patterns on it. The bare part is gilded to display a graceful body. This meticulous statue has followed the custom of carving in Song Dynasty, but also adds something new in its own period. Sakyamuni, originally named Siddhārtha Gautama, was a spiritual teacher from the Indian subcontinent, on whose teachings Buddhism was founded. The "Buddha" means "the awakened one" or "the enlightened one". Buddhism entered China during the Han Dynasty, and the Buddha statue became popular in the Wei and Jin Dynasties. Under such circumstances, it created a carving art and model of the Buddha statue with the unique characteristics of the Chinese nation, which plays an important part in the history of Chinese sculpture.

Painted Carved Zitan Figure of Sakyamuni Buddha in Golden Lacquer

Origin: Ming Dynasty

Height: 94 cm

Hammer Price: RMB 4,032,000

Name of Auction Company: Sungari International

Date of Transaction: 2009-10-19

This big statue has a Buddha and a base which are made from different materials. Carved out of zitan, the Buddha in a kasaya is sitting cross-legged on a lotus throne, with his hands forming the mudra. The lotus throne was adorned with 46 joining bead patterns on its upper edge. With a mound of flesh and pearls on the top, he has a broad forehead, long eyebrows and thin eyes. He lowers his eyes to look down all the livings. The proportion of the body is appropriate. The hair and the mouth are painted in blue and red respectively, and the face and the body are gold. It blends four art styles of India, Nepal, Tibet and the Mainland into one and displays an unusual elegance. It can be dated back to the late 14th Century and the early 15th Century.

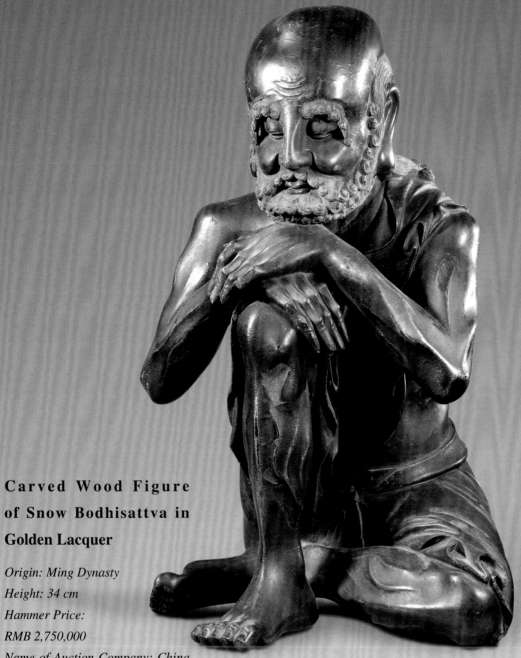

Carved Wood Figure of Snow Bodhisattva in Golden Lacquer

Origin: Ming Dynasty
Height: 34 cm
Hammer Price:
RMB 2,750,000
Name of Auction Company: China
Guardian
Date of Transaction: 2003-11-26

This wood is carved into an elder in full relief. It seems that he is sitting in meditation all alone in remote mountains. The whole design reveals a sense of profound beauty. He curls up one leg, and puts two hands on his right knee to support his head. This old man is very thin, and he has deep eyes, a high nose, and thick beards and eyebrows. The whole body is painted in golden lacquer. The meticulous design, bold and delicate way of cutting, and superb workmanship make it a real model of lacquer crafts.

Carved Zitan Brush Pot with Zoomorphic Patterns

Origin: Ming Dynasty
Height: 14.6 cm
Hammer Price: RMB 2,090,000
Name of Auction Company: China Guardian
Date of Transaction: 2003-11-26

This dark brush pot is carved out of zitan. In the design, kinds of animals appear indistinctly in the rolling sea, such as dragons, lions, horses, tigers, elephants, rhinos, fish and sea snails. The water is torrential, swirling with waves splashing. A circle of flower pattern is carved on the rim of the mouth with various jade inlaid. There are small feet in the bottom. The dense composition and the vigorous way of cutting give us a magnificent and vivid scene of different beasts. This kind of subject had already been used in the Tang and Song Dynasties, and it became more popular in the Yuan and Ming Dynasties.

Carved Boxwood Brush Pot with Patterns by Jiang Fusheng

Origin: Ming Dynasty
Height: 15 cm
Hammer Price: RMB 1,120,000
Name of Auction Company: Chieftown Auction
Date of Transaction: 2009-12-16

This brush pot, shaped in a cylinder, vividly displays a scene that two old men are playing chess under the tree by adopting several carving techniques. In the design, the old man on the right side is thinking with a chess piece between figures; while the left one is smiling with the folded hands hidden in the sleeves, it seems that he is going to win. Behind him, two outsiders who are watching the game seem to have a heated debate. A child is playing on the other side. Small as the figures are, everything is fully equipped. With delicate surroundings like pines, rocks, water and houses, the composition is clear and well-arranged. From the artist's inscription, we can tell that it's a work by Jiang Fusheng, who was a master in wood carving in the late Ming Dynasty.

Carved Huanghuali (Scented Rosewood) Burl Brush Pot

Origin: Ming Dynasty
Height: 19.5 cm
Hammer Price: RMB 1,176,000
Name of Auction Company: Beijing Hanhai
Date of Transaction: 2010-06-06

    With a dignified shape, this Huanghuali (scented rosewood) brush pot, approximated a cylinder, has a thick and warm patina. It is carved out of the natural burls without a trace of modification. Its wood patterns are well-arranged, looking simple and natural. The wood burls had been deeply loved by literati in the late Ming and the early Qing Dynasties, and then proceeded to be a craft. This kind of technique is often used in Huanghuali, which is a kind of rare and precious wood growing in Hainan Island and Vietnam. It is often used to make exquisite furniture in the Ming and Qing Dynasties by literati and officials.

A Qin Made by Zhu Changfang (1608-1646)

Origin: Ming Dynasty
Length: 120 cm
Hammer Price: RMB 286,000
Name of Auction Company: Beijing Hanhai
Date of Transaction: 1998-08-03

A Qin is a seven-stringed plucked instrument played in ancient China. This Qin was made by Zhu Changfang, a relative of an emperor in Ming Dynasty. Zhu inscribed "No.196 made by Luwang in 1634" on it. Both Zhu and the Emperor Qianglong in Qing Dynasty wrote poems on the instrument, making it really a hard-to-get treasure.

The maker, Zhu Changfang, known as Luwang, and also called Jingyi, was good at calligraphy and painting. He was particularly addicted to the Qin. It is said that he had made three hundred Qins. Zhu also wrote a book about Qin's notation.

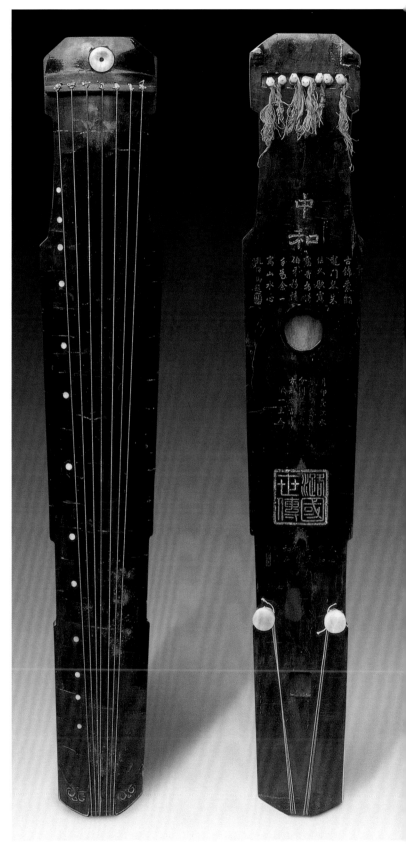

Carved Agalwood Mandarin Duck-shaped Hand Warmer

Origin: Ming Dynasty
Height: 8 cm
Hammer Price: RMB 748,000
Name of Auction Company: China Guardian
Date of Transaction: 2003-11-26

The agalwood, as a rare species of wood, grows in Vietnam, Thailand, India and so on. A few grow in Huian, Fujian Province too. This hand warmer is carved according to the natural shape of a natural agalwood root. This pair of mandarin ducks are tightly clinging to each other on the lotus leaf. It seems that they are whispering softly as mouths slightly opened. The feathers around the neck have distinct gradations. The twin lotus flowers on one stalk imply a meaning of the couple. With an excellent patina, it' s in a perfect size to play with. It can be used to stimulate the circulation of the blood and cause the muscles and joints to relax. And the rubbing action would produce fragrance. This agalwood hand warmer is an uncommon object in full relief in the Qing Dynasty.

Carved Agalwood Brush Pot with "Magpie on Plum Tree" Design

Origin: Early Qing Dynasty

Height: 15.5 cm

Hammer Price: RMB 550,000

Name of Auction Company: China Guardian

Date of Transaction: 2005-05-15

   This brush pot is carved according to the natural shape of the agalwood. On the one side of the wall, there are vivid five-petal plum blossoms on the old and strong trunk in a full bloom. The plum tree with blossoms on the other side is gracefully stretched. The joyful magpies are playing on the tree. The plum blossoms stand for the spring, and the magpie signifies good luck and fortune. The whole design implies that the good fortune has arrived. The novel material, the meticulous design, the realistic expressing way and the superb high relief carving technique are fully presenting the high quality of life of ancient literati. A brush pot in big size like this is really rare due to the scarce material. This one is rated as the highest grade in agalwood carving.

Carved Zitan Brush Pot with Plum Patterns

Origin: Reign of Emperor Kangxi of Qing Dynasty
Height: 18 cm
Hammer Price: RMB 373,650
Name of Auction Company: Hong Kong Christie' s
Date of Transaction: 2001-10-29

Shaped in a cylinder, this brush pot is carved out of Zitan with rigid lines cutting around the rims of the mouth and the bottom. The plum tree is made from mixed copper and the flowers, fruits and butterflies are made of jewelries inlaid. In contrast to the puce patina, the whole picture is fresh and elegant with all these snow-white flowers, red fruits and colorful butterflies. This kind of decoration technique is to inlay the processed materials like various jewelries into the cut space directly on the wood or the lacquer. It had been already used in the Shang and Zhou Dynasties. The refined jewelries, the lifelike design and the exquisite inlay skill make it a real work of art.

Carved Huanghuali Brush Pot with Patterns of Bamboo and Rock by Zhou Zhiyan

Origin: Reign of Emperor Qianlong of Qing Dynasty
Height: 22 cm
Hammer Price: RMB 8,736,000
Name of Auction Company: Beijing Poly
Date of Transaction: 2010-06-04

This brush pot, carved out of the scented rosewood, also known as Huanghuali, has a thick patina. The wall surface was composed of a painting and two poems.   The artist carved a painting with rocks and bamboos on the one side. The composition is simple. In the design, the peculiar rocks and tall bamboos with leaves waving in the wind set each other off beautifully. And on the other side, it is inscribed with two poems written by Zhang Pengchong(1688-1745), who was a Jinshi (metropolitan graduate) in the fifth year of Yongzheng (1727). The artist Zhou Zhiyan is Zhou Hao, the famous carver of Jiading School. This one is his representative work in his art maturity period which is the largest and the most refined and has the longest preface and postscript. The combination of the painting and the poems and the superb workmanship make it an excellent wood carving, let alone the superb carving techniques.

Carved Zitan Brush Pot with Landscape Patterns

Origin: Reign of Emperor Qianlong of Qing Dynasty

Height: 20.5 cm

Hammer Price: RMB 572,000

Name of Auction Company: Beijing Hanhai

Date of Transaction: 2001-12-10

Shaped in a cylinder, this brush pot is carved with a whole picture of scenery of the beautiful Yangtze River in low relief. In pursuit of the Chinese painting effect, the artist carved the open landscape of mountains, water, trees and pavilion in distinct gradations. The composition is well-arranged with simple and smooth cutting lines. The artist engraved and sealed "drawn by Fang Cong" on one side of the painting on the wall surface. Fang Cong (birth and death year unknown), born in Zhejiang Province, was a court painter in the Reign of Emperor Qianlong. With superior quality and rich connotation, this brush pot is a hard-to-get treasure.

Carved Wood Pagodas (one pair)

Origin: Reign of Emperor Qianlong of the Qing Dynasty
Height: 216 cm
Hammer Price: RMB 3,627,744
Name of Auction Company: Hong Kong Sotheby's
Date of Transaction: 2003-10-26

This pair of pagodas used to be a birthday present sent to Emperor Qianlong's mother from nobles or officials in the Qing Dynasty. These two polygon-shaped pagodas, carved out of zitan into the seven-storey tower-style pavilion, are made up of the base, the body and the spire. The body is gradually getting thinner and thinner upward. It has pillars, doors and windows, platforms and railings in each floor. There are 48 niches and 48 Buddhas in total. The huge size, excellent material, meticulous structure and superb workmanship make this pair of pagodas a masterpiece. They were drifted to England 100 years ago and then collected by the famous collector Ma Weidu.

Carved Boxwood Decoration of "Ladies Playing Chess"

Origin: Reign of Emperor Qianlong of Qing Dynasty

Length: 32.6 cm

Hammer Price: RMB 2,240,000

Name of Auction Company: Beijing Poly

Date of Transaction: 2010-12-05

This decoration displays a scene of two ladies playing chess under a tree. In the design, the lady on the right side is in meditation with her body leaning forward and one elbow lifted. The lady on the opposite is going to pick up a piece of chess. The smile shining from her face seems to show that she is going to win. The third lady is playing the flute. Among the illusory fragrant mist from the Boshan incense burner that behind them, it looks just like that they are in the wonderland. The artist carved the tree into a boat form, and then carved the root below it into something like sea waves. This design gives us a feeling that the immortals are shipping on the sea. It implies "plain sailing" or "going up rapidly in the world".

Carved Nanmu Incense Burner, Vase and Box with Bronzy Patterns

Origin: Reign of Emperor Qianlong of Qing Dynasty
Height: 31.8 cm (Burner); 23.4 cm (Vase); 9.4 cm (Box)
Hammer Price: RMB 330,000
Name of Auction Company: Beijing Chengxuan
Date of Transaction: 2006-06-05

This set of fragrant utensils each has an incense burner, a vase and a box. They are all made of Nanmu imitating the bronzy patterns and modelings with three ivorywood bases below. Shaped like a Ding, the burner has two handles with beast heads patterns and flexible rings, a round belly and three legs. The patterns on the burner have four layers with beast mask design on the neck, rectangular spiral design, beast face design, and ruyi design on the belly. The composition is intricate above and simple below. It has a double-deck lid with lotus and ruyi patterns on the surface and a knob with dragon and cloud patterns. Putting the belly with beast face designs as its center, the upper part and the lower part of the vase are carved with same rounds of ruyi patterns, banana leaf patterns and rectangular spiral patterns respectively. Shaped like a cherry-apple, the box and its lid are carved with two different patterns of beast face. The whole set of the fragrant utensils don't need to burn spices inside anymore for their materials are already precious spices.

Carved Jianan Agalwood Hand Beads and a Thumb Ring

Origin: Reigns of Emperor Yongzheng and Qianlong of Qing Dynasty
Length: 26.2 cm(Hand Beads)
Hammer Price: RMB 319,200
Name of Auction Company: Beijing Chengxuan
Date of Transaction: 2008-11-11

This string of hand beads consists of 20 agalwood beads and three decorations with the same material. Small copper beads covered by gold are inlaid on every wood bead. They are arranged into different shapes of the character "Shou", which means "wishing you longevity". The thumb ring is cylindrical with copper covering its interior wall. It used the same decoration technique and material as the hand beads. It brings a distinct contrast between gold and brown. Jianan agalwood is the most rare and precious species in agalwood. During the Reigns of Emperor Yongzheng and Qianlong, officials in Guangdong and Guangxi Provinces used to pay tributes to the emperor like Jianan agalwood hand beads. This set is one of them.

Carved Boxwood Fragrance Holder with Plum Blossom Patterns

Origin: Reign of Emperor Qianlong of Qing Dynasty

Diameter: 8.3 cm

Hammer Price: RMB 392,000

Name of Auction Company: Beijing Poly

Date of Transaction: 2007-12-02

Shaped like the full moon, this fragrance holder is carved out of boxwood. It displays a scene of plum branches with flowers in full bloom and inscribes one poem on each side. The artist gave this round fragrance holder a new connotation of the sun and the moon hanging in the sky together as one. There is no information about the artist Shen Yunshan. From the inscription, we can see this holder was completed in the year 1795, namely the 60th year of the Reign of Emperor Qianlong. Its delicate design and rich connotation rated it the highest kind of the scholar's artwork in ancient China.

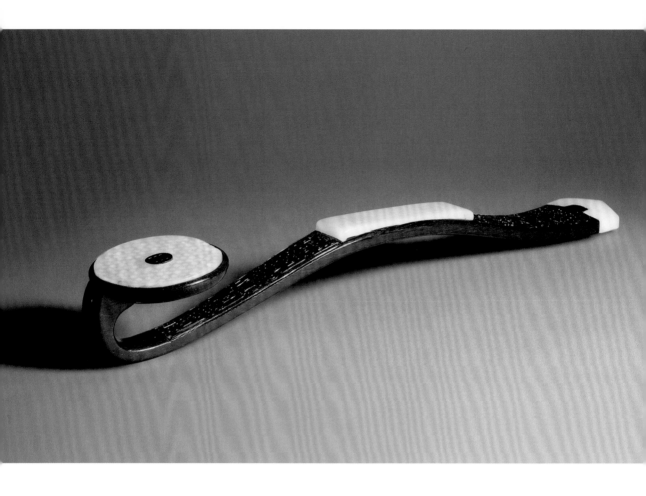

Carved Zitan Ruyi Sceptre of Emperor Qianlong

Origin: Reign of Emperor Qianlong of Qing Dynasty

Length: 39 cm

Hammer Price: RMB 4,290,000

Name of Auction Company: China Guardian

Date of Transaction: 2006-06-03

The ruyi sceptre of Emperor Qianlong, is made of fine zitan hardwood, inlaid with jade from the Han Dynasty at the head, the shaft and the tip, and inlaid in gold and silver with the poetry by the Emperor. Emperor Qianlong loved and adored antiques, and had a good knowledge of antiquities himself. He attached great importance to antique jade in particular. Apart from collecting them, he was good at using antique jade to complement contemporary works of art. He liked choosing antique jade of fine quality or with beautiful patterns for setting in bamboo or wood wares made by the imperial palace workshops (Zaobanchu). For objects of this type, those with imperial inscriptions are of the highest value.

Imperial Carved Zitan Stand and Cover

Origin: Reign of Emperor Qianlong of Qing Dynasty
Length: 16.3 cm
Hammer Price: RMB 9,742,995
Name of Auction Company: New York Christie' s
Date of Transaction: 2009-09-15

The cover and stand are very finely carved overall as a ribbon-tied, brocade-wrapped gift divided into quadrants by the ribbon which is superimposed atop the bow by a rectangular panel carved with the characters "Hu Fu Yan" (crouching tiger inkstone). The quadrants are carved with different scenes of birds in flight above waves from which extend various flowers and grasses, the interior of the cover with a carved and gilded imperial poem referring to the shape of the inkstone followed by the date and two seals, and the top of the stand is carved with a four-character inscription, "Qianlong Yuyong"(for personal use of Qianlong), followed by a four-character seal, "Ji Xia Lin Chi"(a brief moment to practice calligraphy). In the zitan box, there are a flat clay inkstone shaped in a recumbent tiger, and a clay inkstone cover molded in the round as a crouching tiger with its recessed underside inscribed with the same dated Qianlong poem and seals as the cover of the zitan box.

Carved Rosewood Brush Pot with Patterns of Bamboo and Rock

Origin: Mid-Qing Dynasty

Height: 17 cm   Hammer Price: RMB 627,000

Name of Auction Company: Shanghai Jinghua

Date of Transaction: 2004-04-16

This brush pot, shaped in a cylinder, is carved with bamboos and rocks in low relief round the surface. There are two inscriptions engraved nearby the painting. The name "Zhi" mentioned in the first inscription means Zhou Hao. And the writer "Nanhua San Ren" was the famous painter and calligrapher Zhang Pengchong (1688-1745) in the Qing Dynasty. They were contemporaries and both from Jiading. In the inscription, he spoke highly of Zhou Hao. The second said something about how to paint bamboo which was written by Zhou Hao. With both art value and academic value, this brush pot not only builds an elegant artistic conception but also becomes the carrier of presenting different painting views. This brush pot is ascribed to Zhou Hao.

Two Fruit Kernel "Red Cliff" Carvings of a Boat and Sea Creatures

Origin: Reign of Emperor Xianfeng of Qing Dynasty
Length: 4 cm; 4.5 cm
Hammer Price: RMB 291,200
Name of Auction Company: Beijing Council
Date of Transaction: 2007-12-03

By using two superior olive kernels as the material, the "Red Cliff" was carved by Zhan Gusheng, the famous kernel-carving artist in the Qing Dynasty. The upper kernel is carved into a tiny two-storey boat with three cabins. The windows are all available to open and close. There are three people sitting around the table in the front of the boat. The figures in high relief all have clear expressions. It vividly records the scene that Su Dongpo was cruising Yangtze River with his friends. The lower one is carved with sea creature patterns. About 960 words of "Qianhou Chibi Fu" (The Former Red Cliff Rhapsody and The Latter Red Cliff Rhapsody) written by Su Dongpo are all engraved on the bottom of the upper one. The maker, the old Taoist Zhan Gusheng signed that there were 52 people on the boat. It is said that the engraving tools were all self-made and the technique was also unique.

Carved Boxwood Figure of Iron-Crutch Li (Tieguai Li)

Origin: Qing Dynasty
Height: 28 cm

Hammer Price: RMB 2,750,000
Name of Auction Company: Chengming Auction
Date of Transaction: 2007-11-18

By adopting circular carving technique, this boxwood carving brings us a vivid image of Iron-Crutch Li. He seems in meditation with curled eyebrows and beards and shoulder-length hair. He holds the crutch in his two hands and steps his left foot on it. Iron-Crutch Li is said to be the most ancient and popular of the Eight Immortals. He was depicted as a man leaning on a crutch and holding a gourd. It is said that the gourd was full of medicines which he dispensed to the poor and needy to bring dead people back. So the figure of Iron-Crutch Li contains an auspicious meaning of longevity and health.

Carved Boxwood Figure of "Guanyin Sending You a Son" by Zhu Zichang

Origin: Late Qing Dynasty
Height: 26 cm
Hammer Price: RMB 550,000
Name of Auction Company: China Guardian
Date of Transaction: 2006-06-03

This figure is carved out of boxwood in full relief. Guanyin, the Goddess of Mercy, is seen here with a baby in her arms. The composition suggests a well-wish message of fertility. The entire piece is carved exquisitely with an emphasis on the fluidity of the lines, as seen in the bun of hair on Guanyin's head. The base is made from camphorwood in black lacquer. There are two maker's marks with one at the back of the statue and another on the base. The maker Zhu Zichang was an outstanding boxwood carving artist in the late Qing Dynasty. He didn't left many works and this one is his representative work.

Carved Zitan Chop Case with Patterns of Sea and Cloud-Dragon

Origin: Mid-Qing Dynasty
Height: 14 cm
Hammer Price: RMB 165,000
Name of Auction Company: Beijing Hanhai
Date of Transaction: 1995-10-07

By using the rare Zitan hardwood as its material, the artist carved the case with patterns of the mountain, the sea and cloud-dragons on its five faces. In the design, the dragons are flying and jumping in the sky and the rocks in the sea water below are powerful and solid. Every face is circled with the traditional rectangular spiral patterns. The neat style of the case highlights the powerful sea and cloud-dragon as the major part. With the excellent quality, this case must belong to someone noble. The flying dragon implies the dignified status of the Emperor and the flat sea water means it's a peaceful world without conflicts or wars under the emperor's reign. This case has the obvious style and connotation of the court chop case of the Qianlong period. It is really worth collecting.

Carved Zitan Brush Pot by Zhao Zhichen

Origin: Qing Dynasty

Height: 13.2 cm

Hammer Price: RMB 429,000

Name of Auction Company: Shanghai Jinghua

Date of Transaction: 2001-06-23

With clear texture, soft gloss and dark hue, this brush pot is made of Zitan with patterns carved in low relief. In the design, a cluster of orchid shoots is relying on the rocks. It is full of strength and animation with leaves tall and straight and flowers blossomy. The artist' s free way of cutting highlights the charm of the graceful orchid while it and the elegant zitan bring out the best in each other. The artist Zhao Zhichen (1781-1852), born in Qiantang, Zhejiang Province, was the master of seal cutting, painting and calligraphy in the Qing Dynasty.

Carved Boxwood Ganoderma-shaped Water Container and Pen Holder

Origin: Qing Dynasty

Length: 8 cm; 12.6 cm

Hammer Price: RMB 275,000

Name of Auction Company: Shanghai Jinghua

Date of Transaction: 2003-08-24

By adopting several techniques like relief carving and piercing, these water containers and pen holders are both carved into two clusters of twisted branches with ganodermas in different sizes and shapes. A hole dug upward in the center of the water container is used to hold water, while the pen holder stretches transversely. The twisting, wrinkles, holes and burls on the surface of the branches and the texture of the cap are all skillfully imitated as to be indistinguishable from the original. The delicate design, the unique modeling and the super workmanship make it a rare work of art in the scholar's studio.

Carved Arenga Pinnata Plate

Origin: Qing Dynasty
Diameter: 23.5 cm
Hammer Price: RMB 165,000
Name of Auction Company:
China Guardian
Date of Transaction: 2003-11-26

This plate, made of arenga pinnata, has an open mouth and a flat bottom. The modeling is simple, and the patterns covered on it are natural without any modification. The fishroe-shaped dots are covered at the bottom densely. The round spots on the exterior wall are similar to the cutting scars of bamboo root. That is why it is always to be considered as a bamboo root production, while it's exactly a natural pattern of arenga pinnata after polishing. Only a few of the arenga pinnata woodworks are left due to its scarce material. Some are preserved in the Palace Museum now, and few of them are even inscribed with the Emperor Qianlong's poems. It is thus obvious that how precious arenga pinnata woodworks were at that time.

Carved Boxwood Sculpture of "Reading to Grandmother"

Origin: Modern Time

Height: 19 cm

Hammer Price: RMB 560,000

Name of Auction Company: China Guardian

Date of Transaction: 2007-05-12

This is a delicately carved and fully rounded sculpture of two expressively postured figures. The old woman sits with her face wrinkled and her hair pulled back dressing simply Her knees are squared, with her right elbow resting on her right knee with a fine pipe in hand, and her left arm around the back of the young girl wearing in a red scarf and with pigtails, who leans against the woman's leg and looks up at her excitedly while reading. This sculpture is carved out of a light yellow wood of warm tone. It has a raised wooden base, with characters "Reading to Grandmother" engraved at the center. The artist Ruan Baoguang (1925.7-), born in Fuzhou, Fujian Province, is the leading carver of ivory figure carving in China.

Mould-Pressing Gourd-shaped Vase with Patterns of "Fu" and "Shou"

Origin: Reign of Emperor Kangxi of Qing Dynasty
Height: 26 cm
Hammer Price: RMB 330,000
Name of Auction Company: China Guardian
Date of Transaction: 1996-10-21

This vase is shaped like a special gourd with a square upper belly and an irregular octahedron lower belly. Pattern of "Shou" (longevity) is carved on the front face of both bellies, while other patterns like ruyi and peach are also carved on the lower one. It implies an auspicious meaning of "living well and long". Flower pattern is carved in the center of the bottom and four characters are inscribed on each corner reading "Kang Xi Shang Wan" (enjoyed by the Emperor Kangxi). A circle of hawksbill covered the rim of the mouth. The unique modeling, the elegant pattern and the ingenious mould make it a relatively rarely-seen fine work of gourd in the Qing Dynasty. A little part was eaten by moths.

Mould-Pressing Gourd-shaped Burner with Patterns of Taotie

Origin: Reign of Emperor Qianlong of Qing Dynasty

Height: 21 cm

Hammer Price: RMB 385,000

Name of Auction Company: China Guardian

Date of Transaction: 1997-04-18

Imitating the modeling of a bronze gu in the Shang and Zhou Dynasties, this burner has a wide flared mouth, a vertical rim, a contracted neck, a swelling belly and a false circular foot. Black lacquer covered the inside and patterns of stylized lotus petal and taotie were molded around the exterior surface of the burner. Four characters are inscribed on it reading "Kang Xi Shang Wan" (enjoyed by the Emperor Kangxi). This kind of mould-pressing gourd-shaped burner is relatively rare, which makes it a really hard-to-get work of art.

Ⅲ. Ivory Carvings

Carved Ivory Figure of Sakyamuni Buddha

Origin: Song Dynasty
Height: 19.8 cm   Hammer Price: RMB 7,840,000
Name of Auction Company: Beijing Council
Date of Transaction: 2008-12-08

  This ivory statue is made of a whole quality ivory in full relief. The ivory used is fine, smooth, natural and with dense grain. The Buddha statue is dignified and natural. Clothes and ornaments of the Buddha are carved with smooth knife-carving techniques. As we all know, ivory is natural protein in texture and is hard to preserve. Ivory carvings of the Song Dynasty are ever more precious.

Ivory Carving Figure of Guanyin

Origin: Ming Dynasty
Height: 30.3 cm
Hammer Price: RMB 605,000
Name of Auction Company: Beijing Hanhai
Date of Transaction: 1995-04-12

This ivory statue is made of a whole quality ivory. The ivory is of fine texture and bright luster. The Buddha wears her hair in a bun with her graceful and plump face slightly towards left, smiling. Wearing a vestment with a dress underneath, the Buddha is elegant and charming. The using of blade and file displays the strength of lines. It is a masterpiece with skilled craftsmanship and high quality ivory.

Ivory Carving of the God of Longevity and His Deer

Origin: Reign of Emperor Hongzhi of Ming Dynasty
Height: 19 cm
Hammer Price: RMB 258,500
Name of Auction Company: Shanghai Xinren
Date of Transaction: 2004-12-08

The statue depicts the God of Longevity sitting cross-legged, with a lying deer leaning close to him. The God of Longevity is also referred to as the Canopus, who takes charge of people's lifetime, the symbol of longevity. The deer, a symbol of "Lu", means prosperity literally. Therefore it implies the pursuit towards happiness among Chinese. The adopting of powerful lines and fine polish is the style of the Ming Dynasty.

Carved Ivory Brush Pot

Origin: Ming Dynasty

Height: 15.8 cm

Hammer Price: RMB 115,500

Name of Auction Company: China Guardian

Date of Transaction: 2000-05-08

    This brush pot is made of a whole ivory. With characteristics of a thick material, a soft yellow color and a natural texture, the pot seemed more elegant and pure which was deeply loved by literati. The natural trace of aging is the witness of long years which makes it an artwork with both history value and artistic value. It' s really hard to preserve it from the Ming Dynasty. This is the only one ivory brush pot of the Ming Dynasty among the top ten ivory brush pots in the auction market. The scarce amount would make it a much higher price if it reappears in the market after a decade.

Ivory Carving Figure of a Beautiful Lady

Origin: Late Ming and Early Qing Dynasties
Height: 64 cm
Hammer Price: RMB 638,000
Name of Auction Company: Shanghai Jinghua
Date of Transaction: 2007-07-14

The statue depicts a beautiful lady, wearing her hair high in a bun with a hairpin like a lucid ganoderma. The lady is in a wide sleeve gown with a waistband down and a graceful dress, standing on a stone. She lifts her dress with left hand and raises her right hand with a scroll in it. The statue vividly reflects the real life with a skilled workmanship. The statue consists of two parts — the lady and the stone, and is connected by a tenon. Till today, it is well preserved.

Ivory Carving Figure of Madonna

Origin: Early Qing Dynasty
Height: 37 cm
Hammer Price: RMB 113,531
Name of Auction Company: London Christie' s
Date of Transaction: 2005-07-12

This ivory statue is carved with smooth lines by using superb craftsmanship. The expression of the Madonna is kind and elegant, holy and amiable. The tradition of ivory carving of Madonna dates back to the 14th century in Europe, and it is introduced to China in the late Ming Dynasty. It reflects the missionaries' coming also brought the western thoughts into China. The ivory statue is the evidence of the culture exchange between China and the western.

Carved Ivory Brush Pot in Black Lacquer

Origin: Reign of Emperor Kangxi of Qing Dynasty
Height: 9.7 cm
Hammer Price: RMB 715,000
Name of Auction Company: Beijing Hanhai
Date of Transaction: 2000-12-11

Shaped in a cylinder, this brush pot has small feet with rectangular spiral patterns carved around the rims of both the mouth and the bottom. The surface of the brush pot is carved with five-petal plum blossoms on the winding branches. A poem and two maker's marks are inscribed beside the plums. This kind of technique is to carve the patterns on the surface of the ivory in low relief firstly, and then paint multi-layer black lacquer on blank spaces to make it the same level with the patterns and polish at last. Ivory carvings in the Reign of Emperor Kangxi are rare in the collections of the palace, let alone the auction market. Therefore, this one is especially a treasure.

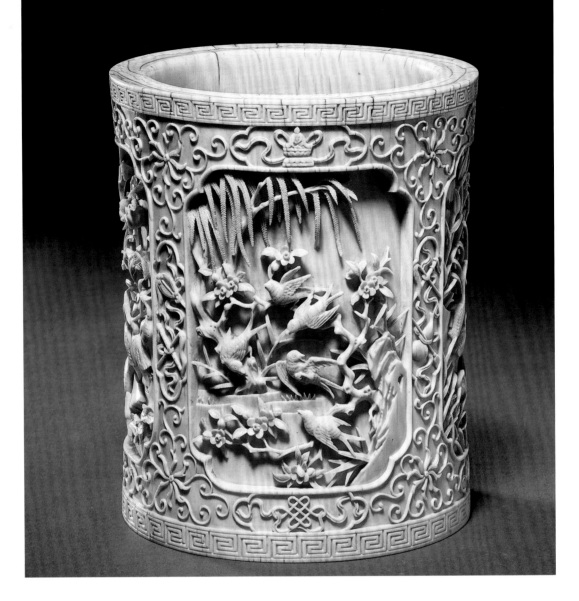

Carved Ivory Brush Pot with Patterns of Flowers and Birds of Four Seasons

Origin: Reigns of Emperor Yongzheng and Qianlong of Qing Dynasty
Height: 14.2 cm
Hammer Price: RMB 2,296,000
Name of Auction Company: Beijing Chengxuan
Date of Transaction: 2009-11-22

Shaped in a cylinder, this brush pot is made of the ivory of fine texture and mild luster. It is carved with rectangular spiral patterns in intaglio on the rims of both the mouth and the bottom. Patterns of flowers and birds of four seasons are carved among the lotus twig and eight-treasure patterns. In the design, the flowers are swaying and birds are dancing. It's a treasure with well-arranged composition, fresh style and excellent way of cutting. It has the same typical style with that of the court workmanship during the flourishing age of Qing Dynasty. Therefore, it should be a product made by a Cantonese ivory carver from the Ivory Workshops belonging to the imperial palace workshops (Zaobanchu) located in the Forbidden City.

Carved Ivory Water Container of "Monkeys Climbing Peach"

Origin: Reign of Emperor Qianlong of Qing Dynasty

Diameter: 7.5 cm

Hammer Price: RMB 101,200

Name of Auction Company: China Guardian

Date of Transaction: 2003-07-13

The water container is used for holding water to add to the inkstone. The body of the container is shaped like a big peach, and it also has a peach branch-shaped handle with leaves stretched and small peaches on. Three small monkeys are climbing the big peach. There is a tiny ivory spoon carved in the shape of a peach with a ganoderma-shaped handle. A carved wood base in the same style is equipped. Its unique modeling, fine material, bright and pure luster and excellent workmanship compose a rare work of art of ivory carving in the scholar's studio. There is no such kind of collection at present which exactly gives it a good prospect.

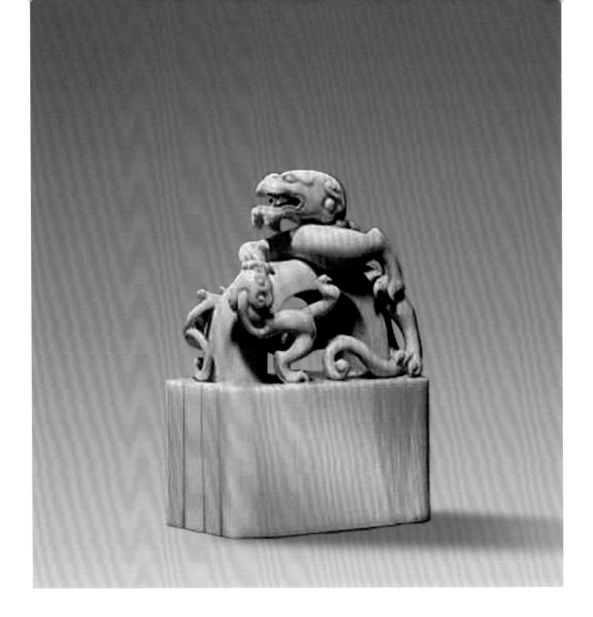

Imperial Carved Ivory Seal

Origin: Reign of Emperor Qianlong of Qing Dynasty
Length of Side: 5.9 cm
Hammer Price: RMB 3,083,500
Name of Auction Company: Hong Kong Sotheby's
Date of Transaction: 2009-10-08

This seal is made of a cream-colored ivory with a natural patina, a rectangular section and rounded vertical corners, carved with two Chi dragons clambering on the top of the loop handle. The finely carved larger dragon perches atop with its sinuous body wrapped around the loop, with the smaller dragon emerging from under the loop and looking up at the larger beast. The seal face is engraved in positive seal script reading "Yi Shanshui Wenji Ziyu" (to enjoy oneself with landscape and books). The strength of the carving is shown by the sturdy limbs and dynamic postures of the two Chi dragons which masterly capture the spirit of the beast.

Carved Ivory Figures with Colored Enamel (one pair)

Origin: Reign of Emperor Qianlong of Qing Dynasty

Height: 72 cm; 71 cm

Hammer Price: RMB 10,580,000

Name of Auction Company: Sotheby's

Date of Transaction: 2001-11-14

Both supported by a rosewood Xumi base, these two ivory figures are getting down to one knee with one holding high the Conch Shell and the other the Parasol. They look solemn. Both the Conch Shell and the Parasol are one of the eight auspicious symbols of Buddhism. The Conch Shell represents the thoughts of the Buddha to awaken living beings from the deep slumber of ignorance and urge them to accomplish their own and others' welfare, while the Parasol represents the crown and the dignified Buddha Dharma protecting the whole world. The figures are Mongolians in ancient China according to their faces, hair styles and costumes. This pair of artworks have the typical features of court workmanship in Qianlong Reign.

Carved Ivory Decoration of Figures

Origin: Reign of Emperor Qianlong of Qing Dynasty

Height: 17.8 cm

Hammer Price: RMB 504,000

Name of Auction Company: Beijing Hanhai

Date of Transaction: 2007-06-25

Once belonged to the imperial palace, this work of art is made of fine ivory. In the design, a beautiful lady is smiling and looking directly forward with her left hand on her back, while the right hand is raised with a fan holding beside the shoulder. A cute boy is leaning against the piling-up stones and lifting his right arm to play with the parrot. The base is made of zitan wood with lotus petal patterns. By adopting circular carving technique, this work of art is small and exquisite. It' s a fine work of art with an extremely dense artistic style of the court.

Carved Ivory "Three Sheep" Incense Holder

Origin: Reign of Emperor Qianlong of Qing Dynasty
Height: 7.8 cm
Hammer Price: RMB 918,400
Name of Auction Company: Beijing Poly
Date of Transaction: 2010-06-04

Using fine ivory as the material, this incense holder has a double-lip mouth, a square bottom and a standardized four-edge body with concise patterns and a fitted brocade box. On the top of the holder, three sheep are carved in full relief with their eyes inlaid with rhinoceros horn and amber. The design of three sheep of one mother and two children is full of tender feeling. The moral of this modeling is "San Yang Kai Tai" (the spring comes in full form). But it not only means the beginning of the spring but also has auspicious meaning of flourish and prosperity. The patterns on the body also symbolize the harmony of Yin Yang and the society. The entire modeling is delicate and of primitive simplicity with a warm patina. This kind of hollowed out objects were widely used in the palace and officials' homes to purify air in the Qing Dynasty.

Imperial Ivory Gourd-shaped Incense Holder with a Long Chain

Origin: Reign of Emperor Qianlong of Qing Dynasty

Height: 8 cm

Hammer Price: RMB 1,456,000

Name of Auction Company: Beijing Poly

Date of Transaction: 2007-12-02

This ivory incense holder is shaped like a gourd with a contracted waist. Rectangular spiral designs are pierced on the upper and the lower bellies. With swastika patterns (卍) on the waist, the rest part is carved with kui (a one-legged monster in fable) patterns. Five bats in a circle are on the bottom with a round "shou" pattern inside which implies longevity. A vivid pedicel-shaped lid is on the top of the holder with a main chain linked to the body. Three short chains are attached to it with small pendants of a gourd, a basket and a bell. "Hulu", the pronunciation of gourd is similar to "Fulu" in Chinese, while the latter means good fortune and prosperity. The chain also has a meaning of "continuing forever". The incense holder is equipped with an ancient fitted wooden box of the late Qing Dynasty.

Carved Ivory Food Carrier

Origin: Reign of Emperor Qianlong of Qing Dynasty
Height: 54 cm   Hammer Price: RMB 1,540,000
Name of Auction Company: Beijing Council
Date of Transaction: 2006-11-23

This ivory food carrier carved with the Eight Immortals, is a product made by a Cantonese ivory carver from the Ivory Workshops belonging to the imperial palace workshops (Zaobanchu) located in the Forbidden City. Consisting of a cover, a basketry of three layers, a base and a handle, the whole body is made up of 46 pieces of ivory by applying many techniques, such as piercing, openwork carving and relief carving into the combination. Clustering around the top of the cover, six colored frames, from top to bottom, are linking up those ivories together. The cover, with a vase-shaped crown in the centre, resembles an official headgear in the Qing Dynasty. As for its base, each face is groups of with patterns of grass and flower through the hollow engraving. The handle is engraved with group celestials and the Eight Immortals of Taoism in different gestures. With its exquisite knife-carving technique and lucid and live style, it stands for the great achievement of the ivory carving in the Qing Dynasty.

Carved Ivory Bowl with a Lid

Origin: Reign of Emperor Qianlong of Qing Dynasty
Diameter: 11.4 cm
Hammer Price: RMB 1,456,000
Name of Auction Company: Beijing Hanhai
Date of Transaction: 2010-12-11

    This round bowl has an open mouth, a ring foot with pierced patterns of twining twigs. There are no patterns or decorations inside the bowl. Peach and its blossoms on branches are carved on the lid and red bats dancing among the flowers are carved on the exterior surface of the bowl. In traditional Chinese culture, peach is considered as the fruit of heaven which would bring longevity, and "Fu", the pronunciation of bat is the same as "Fu" (good fortune) and "Fu" (wealth), which makes it also an auspicious symbol. Clusters of flowers and leaves are well-arranged around the surface of the bowl. Smooth and delicate silver plates are inlaid inside the bowl and the lid. The shape and the skill of carving, polishing and dyeing are all with typical features of ivory carvings made in the imperial palace workshops (Zaobanchu). There is another one with the same design which is preserved in the Palace Museum now.

Ivory Pomegranates Carving (one pair)

Origin: Qing Dynasty (18th Century)
Width: 10.5 cm (single)
Hammer Price: RMB 597,040
Name of Auction Company: Hong Kong Christie' s
Date of Transaction: 2010-05-31

Using fine ivory as the material, this pair of works of art adopt several techniques like circular carving, low relief carving and piercing. Each naturally is modeled as a pomegranate fruit bursting to expose the pink seeds within, put on a gnarled stem with further smaller fruits and blooms. The pomegranate is a symbol of fertility. There are bat patterns in high relief carved on the pomegranates. With the same pronunciation as "Fu" (good fortune) in Chinese, people often use it as an auspicious symbol. It is more than a masterpiece with such superlative craftsmanship.

Carved Ivory Brush Pot with Patterns of Sea and Cloud-dragon

Origin: Mid-Qing Dynasty
Height: 14.5 cm   Hammer Price: RMB 308,000
Name of Auction Company: Beijing Hanhai
Date of Transaction: 2001-12-10

    The brush pot is made of a section of hollowed-out ivory. Flames, clouds, waves are carved on its exterior surface. A dragon is soaring up and down indistinctly in the waves and clouds. The dragon is covered with scales. With glaring eyes, an open mouth, flowing hair, sharp claws and hard tail feathers, the strong dragon is hovering vigorously. It seems to have grand power of an unbeatable king. In the thick and solid ivory, the flames, clouds and waves were engraved at three layers in different height. The dragon is flying in the three layers, which brings three-dimensional effect and magnificent momentum. Engraved with skillful and excellent technique, it seems that the flame is erupting, the clouds are driven by wind and the sound of waves pounding the bank can be heard. All of these show that the brush pot is made by a dab hand. The superior material, elaborate skill and dense emblazonry are all with typical features of sculptures made in Beijing in the mid-Qing Dynasty.

Carved Ivory Brush Pot Made by Laigong

Origin: Mid-Qing Dynasty
Height: 12.1 cm
Hammer Price: RMB 363,000
Name of Auction Company: Shanghai Chongyuan
Date of Transaction: 2003-04-20

Shaped in a cube with round corners, this brush pot consists of a body, an affixed baseboard and four small feet. The four sides are made of a whole ivory without any ornamentation on it, which highlights the natural texture of the ivory. There is a poem inscribed on one side of the pot with a maker's mark reading "Made by Laigong in the Autumn of 1707". The ivory baseboard has natural texture of circularity. The simple style makes it a rare elegant work of art in the scholar's studio. In the auction market, the more exquisite or complex ivory object of scholar's studio would often have higher prices. But it sometimes received a sky-high price for its simplicity. This one is well illustrated.

Ivory Basket (one pair)

Origin: Mid-Qing Dynasty
Height: 20.5 cm
Hammer Price: RMB 896,000
Name of Auction Company: Beijing Council
Date of Transaction: 2008-05-21

This pair of baskets was perfectly carved by a Cantonese ivory craftsman. Shaped in octagon, the lid and the basketry consisting of 8 hollowed-out plates have eight feet with patterns of ruyi and ganoderma. The process of the craftsmanship is firstly to carve ivory into slices with refined patterns as thin as hair and then splice them together. There are hundreds of small ivory slices with hollowed-out patterns carved on every joint and rim. On the top of the lid, a stereoscopic pattern of a phoenix kissing the magnolia flower is carved in full relief. Without any traces of unsuccessful cutting, this pair of baskets is definitely one of the best ivory artworks.

Ivory Statue of the Emperor Yongzheng

Origin: Reign of Emperor Jiaqing of Qing Dynasty
Height: 29.2 cm   Hammer Price: RMB 275,000
Name of Auction Company: Beijing Hanhai
Date of Transaction: 2005-06-20

    This ivory statue has won its applause for its elegant and dignified style. Wearing the imperial dragon robe and court beads, Emperor Yongzheng is sitting on the throne with peaceful and dignified expression. Cloud-dragon patterns in hollow engraving are carved on the throne. A wood base supports the statue with sliver inlaid and patterns in enamel. On the bottom of the statue, there are two marks in intaglio reading "Yongzheng Yu Rong" (appearance of Emperor Yongzheng) and "Jiaqing Gengshen Jing Zhi" (made in 1800). The statue has a fine and complex workmanship, and its figure and patterns have followed the calligraphic style with composition well-arranged. This kind of ivory statue is really a rare treasure handed down from age to age.

Ivory Seal with Dragon Handles (one pair)

Origin: Reign of Emperor Tongzhi of Qing Dynasty

Height: 11 cm

Hammer Price: RMB 484,000

Name of Auction Company: Shanghai Xinren

Date of Transaction: 2004-12-08

This pair of seals is shaped in elliptic cylinder with dignified dragons clambering on each top of them. Hundreds of small characters of "Fu" and "Shou" with two big ones are respectively carved on the front surface of each seal. The inscriptions in double-lines regular script read "Happy Birthday to Governor-general Li Hongzhang in His Fifty" and "Congratulatiing by Subordinate Zeng Jize". And two lines from the poem "Shuxiang" of Du Fu are carved on the seal face. Zeng Jize, the elder son of Zeng Guofan, presented this pair of seals to Li Hongzhang as a 50th birthday gift in 1873. According to the research, on his 60th birthday in 1883, Li Hongzhang, already the grand secretary, asked the great carver Yu shuo to add "Qianhou Chushibiao" on the back surfaces of the seals to compare himself to Zhu Geliang to show his resolution of doing his best to serve the country.

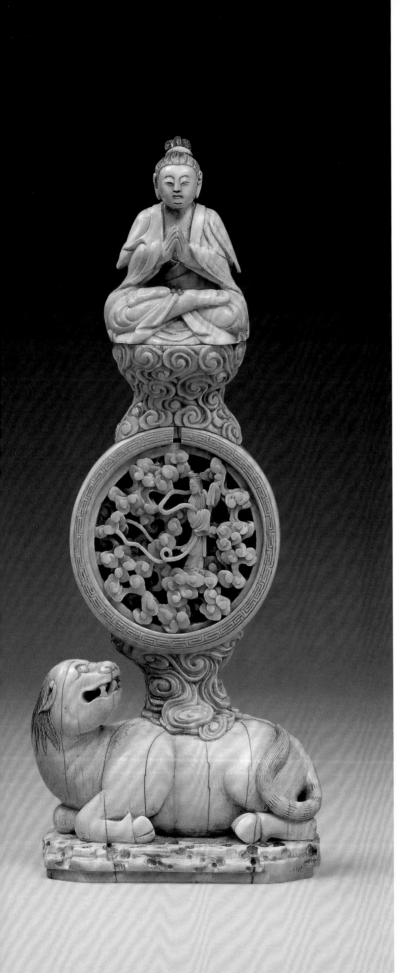

Ivory Carving of Auspicious Animal and Water-Moon Guanyin

Origin: Qing Dynasty
Height: 23 cm
Hammer Price: RMB 220,000
Name of Auction Company: Sungari International
Date of Transaction: 2002-12-07

This work is carved out of ivory with a suanni (lion) as the base. Shaped like a lion, suanni, is the fourth out of the nine sons of dragon. Crouching down on the ground, it is turning its head back with four round limbs and a long tail on the buttocks. Above the suanni, an auspicious cloud upbears a round screen carved with patterns of fairy maiden and immortal travelling separately. There is a Guanyin sitting on the top with palms together devoutly. It seems that she is looking at all the livings below. The superb combination of circular carving, hollow engraving and relief carving makes it a rare work of art.

Colored Ivory Carving of Lu Star

Origin: Qing Dynasty
Height: 29 cm
Hammer Price: RMB 242,000
Name of Auction Company: Beijing Hanhai
Date of Transaction: 2001-07-02

This is an excellent work adopting several carving techniques like circular carving, hollow engraving and relief carving and so on. In the design, the Lu Star is standing on a thick and square base with small green railings. He is feeding a ganoderma to a cute deer crouching on his arm. Wearing a blue robe and cloth shoes, he is smiling peacefully. It has fine and smooth cutting lines, vivid expressions and clothes, rich colors and an auspicious meaning.

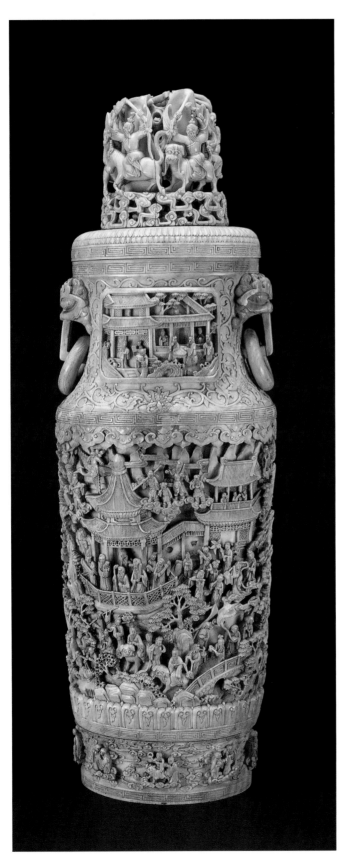

Carved Ivory Vase Illustrating "Groups of Immortals Offering Birthday Congratulations"

Origin: Qing Dynasty
Height: 48 cm
Hammer Price: RMB 605,000
Name of Auction Company: Tianjin Emperor's Ferry
Date of Transaction: 2000-11-07

With fine texture and antique luster, this vase has a lid and two hanging rings with different kinds of exquisite patterns carved on the whole body, such as animals, pavilions, running water, bridges, trees, flowers and groups of immortals. It is really ingenious and intricate that the artist adopted a combination of several carving skills to carve more than ten layers of the patterns. Although so many different figures are involved, the composition is well-arranged. The wonderful workmanship of this treasure has already excelled nature.

Ivory Carving Armrest with Human Figures and Landscape

Origin: Qing Dynasty
Height: 30.1 cm
Hammer Price: RMB 250,000
Name of Auction Company: Beijing Hanhai
Date of Transaction: 2002-12-09

Armrest is a stationery used by the ancient people to be put under the arm to practice the calligraphy. This item used to be collected by the royal family. It is carved like a bamboo joint in a tile shape with four short feet. The front side is carved with seven kids flying the kite. The back side is carved with people traveling in the mountain and stream area.

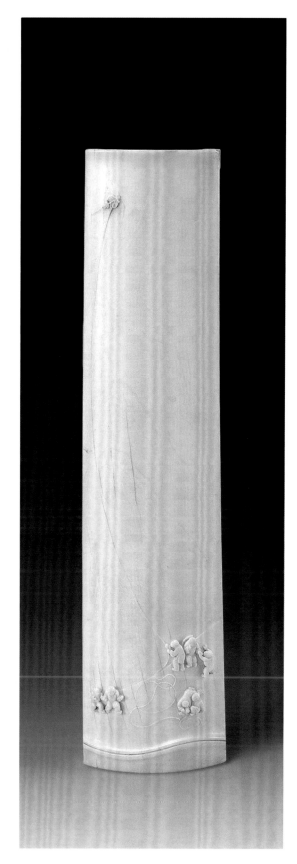

Ivory Carving Brush Inkslab with Longevity, Flower and Fruit Patterns

Origin: Qing Dynasty

Length: 16.8 cm

Hammer Price: RMB 110,000

Name of Auction Company: Beijing Hanhai

Date of Transaction: 2005-06-20

The brush inkslab is shaped in a plate which looks like a persimmon fruit. Inside the plate, a bat is facing a ruyi and ready for flying. A peach branch stretches its leaves along the edge of the plate with a peach fruit on it. The techniques of circular carving, piercing and relief carving make this item a real masterpiece.

Ivory Ruyi with Ganoderma and Pine Patterns

Origin: Qing Dynasty
Length: 32 cm
Hammer Price: RMB 187,000
Name of Auction Company: Shanghai Jinghua
Date of Transaction: 2001-06-23

This ruyi is in chestnut color with fine texture. The head part is carved into a ganoderma in full relief. The handle part is carved into a pine stem which also has four different sized ganodermas growing on it. Pine needles also can be found on it. With the elegant craftsmanship and unique style, this item is a masterpiece of ivory carving.

Ivory Carving Basket

Origin: Qing Dynasty
Height: 30 cm
Hammer Price: RMB 672,000
Name of Auction Company: Chieftown Auction
Date of Transaction: 2007-11-04

This basket is shaped in an oval. Both the cover and the basketry are knitted of thin ivory strips by transpiercing, thrusting, bending and jointing them together. The knob is carved into a peach. The handle is pierced into flowers and leaves as a whole. The edges of the cover and the body are carved in round pattern. The foot part is pierced with patterns of twining flowers. This item was used by the Qing Royal Court to carry flowers which represents the highly developed ivory craftsmanship of that time.

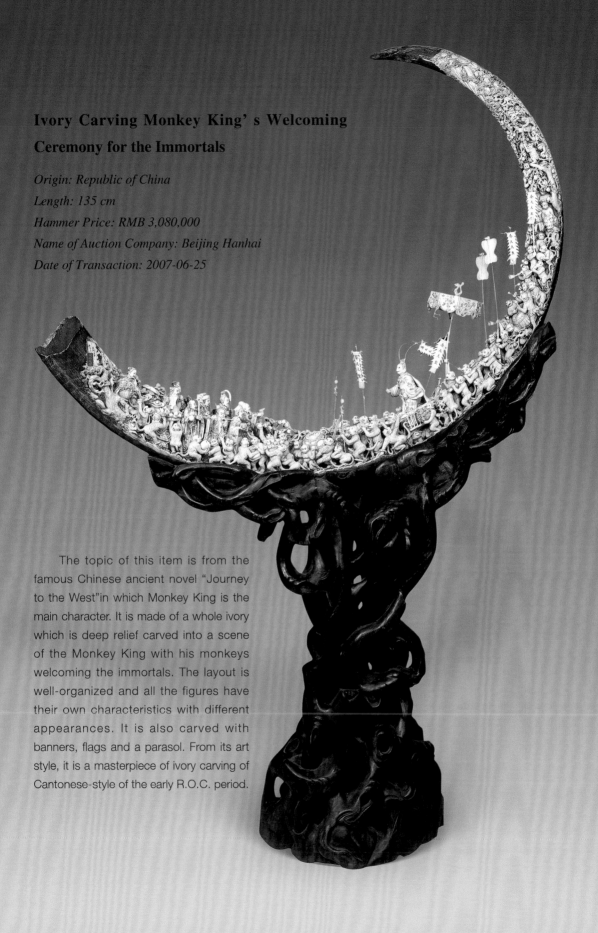

Ivory Carving Monkey King's Welcoming Ceremony for the Immortals

Origin: Republic of China

Length: 135 cm

Hammer Price: RMB 3,080,000

Name of Auction Company: Beijing Hanhai

Date of Transaction: 2007-06-25

The topic of this item is from the famous Chinese ancient novel "Journey to the West"in which Monkey King is the main character. It is made of a whole ivory which is deep relief carved into a scene of the Monkey King with his monkeys welcoming the immortals. The layout is well-organized and all the figures have their own characteristics with different appearances. It is also carved with banners, flags and a parasol. From its art style, it is a masterpiece of ivory carving of Cantonese-style of the early R.O.C. period.

Ivory Carving Chinese Cabbage with Katydids Made by Yang Shihui

Origin: Modern Time
Length: 29 cm
Hammer Price: RMB 392,000
Name of Auction Company: China Guardian
Date of Transaction: 2009-09-12

This item was made of a fine solid ivory during the Anti-Japanese War period. The main part is carved into a Chinese cabbage which has clear layers and veins. In the middle of its top, there are two katydids confronted with their palpi and alae opened. There are ladybirds, a praying mantis and crickets watching around. A morning-glory is stretching and twisting. The bottorm has an inscription"Carved by Run Sheng"which suggests that it is a product made by the ivory carving master .

Ivory Carving Fan with Longevity Pattern

Origin: Modern Time
Height: 127cm
Hammer Price: RMB 176,000
Name of Auction Company: Shanghai Dongfang
Date of Transaction: 2002-12-02

The total height of this item is 127cm and the height of the main fan part is 60cm. The whole structure absorbs the merits of the traditional Chinese frame structure to show the art creativity. It has a frame with longevity pattern and dragon pattern to support the core part. The core part is deep relief carved with a fairy and a crane on one side and a God of Longevity on the other side. It has a chain linked with three ivory balls which are carved with different Chinese characters for celebrating the longevity and other lucky patterns.

IV. Horn Carvings

Rhinoceros Horn Cup Shaped in Buffalo Head

Origin: Song Dynasty

Length: 8 cm

Hammer Price: RMB 2,240,000

Name of Auction Company: Beijing Poly

Date of Transaction: 2010-12-05

This rhino horn cup is shaped in a buffalo head, with round eyes and a nose with a hole which can tie the rope to take it. The barrel is drilled very well and smoothly. It is put on an ivory base. The cup is in a simple style, but still we can see the great craftsmanship.

Rhinoceros Horn Cup Shaped in Flower

Origin: Early Ming Dynasty

Height: 25 cm

Hammer Price: RMB 2,750,000

Name of Auction Company: Beijing Hanhai

Date of Transaction: 2006-06-26

This rhino horn cup is made from transparent material, coloring like amber. It is shaped in a flower with the pistil inside. The outer wall is relief carved with vines, leaves and flowers which is crisscross with each other. To match the main part, the base is made of zitan which also carved into vines with flowers. It is a rear big rhino horn carving item of the early Ming Dynasty.

Rhinoceros Horn Cup with Dragon and Phoenix Patterns Made by Bao Tiancheng

Origin: Reign of Emperor Wanli of Ming Dynasty
Height: 14.2 cm
Hammer Price: RMB 11,200,000
Name of Auction Company: Beijing Poly
Date of Transaction: 2010-12-05

This cup with a comparatively big size, fine quality material, good design and exquisite craftsmanship, is an outstanding rhino horn carving product. It is made of Sumatran rhino horn which colors in deep date red. The cup body is carved with dragon patterns which is similar with a rhino horn kettle collected in the Palace Museum. As it was made for the Royal Court, it has very delicate carving patterns. The mouth of the cup is also carved with dragon patterns which has the typical Ming style. The body is embedded with an ivory chip with the inscription"Made in the Reign of Emperor Wanli of the Ming Dynasty" on it. It also has a "Bao Tiancheng" inscription inside the patterns which suggests it is made by the famous horn carving craftsman Bao Tiancheng himself.

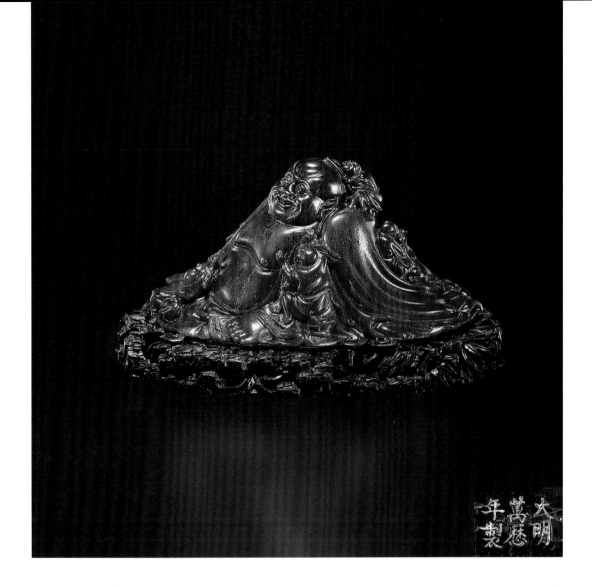

Rhinoceros Horn Bag Monk Statue with Five Children

Origin: Reign of Emperor Wanli of Ming Dynasty
Width: 15 cm Weight: 262 g
Hammer Price: RMB 5,019,080
Name of Auction Company: Hong Kong Christie' s
Date of Transaction: 2008-05-27

This item is made of fine rhino horn with exquisite craftsmanship. It is carved into the Cloth Bag Monk who has a happy appearance in full relief. On his shoulders, two sides, the front and the back, it is carved with five vivid children playing with him. The story is originated from the Five Dynasties period that five sons from one family all successively passed the Imperial Examination. People believed that the Cloth Bag Monk is an incarnation of Maitreya and a symbol of happiness.

Rhinoceros Horn Gong on an Ivory Base

Origin: Reign of Emperor Wanli of Ming Dynasty

Diameter: 6.7 cm

Hammer Price: RMB 220,000

Name of Auction Company: Beijing Hanhai

Date of Transaction: 1996-06-30

This rhino horn gong is put on an ivory base. It has no decorative pattern but is inscribed with a poem which said that the Rhino horn gong could send message to the heaven like a bugle. The texture of the horn is hard and the color is like the amber. It can expel the evil spirit and calm the angry. If you drink wine from it, you can extend your longevity. This item is a birthday gift sent by Zhou Tianqiu to Lu Zhi, both of them were famous artists in the late Ming Dynasty.

Rhinoceros Horn Bowl Carved with Amida Buddha

Origin: Reign of Emperor Wanli of Ming Dynasty

Diameter: 15cm

Hammer Price: RMB 1,210,000

Name of Auction Company: Beijing Hanhai

Date of Transaction: 2004-11-22

    This item is made of fine rhinoceros material, with an open mouth, a curving wall and a round foot. It has a smooth body, carved with four regular script characters "E Mi Tuo Fo" meaning Amida Buddha. Between every two characters, it is relief carved with four arhats with different appearances who sit on the lotus thrones. On the bottom, it has an inscription "Donated by Mi Wanzhong, in front of the Buddha in the Cave of Vajra, Jiuhua Mountain, in the Year of Jihai, Wanli Reign". Mi Wanzhong was a famous artist in the Ming Dynasty who enjoys equal popularity with Dong Qichang.

Rhinoceros Horn Buddha Statue

Origin: Ming Dynasty
Height: 15.5cm
Hammer Price: RMB 5,500,000
Name of Auction Company: North Latitude
Date of Transaction: 2009-11-22

This item is carved out of an Asian rhino horn. Following its natural shape, it is carved into a Buddha statue which has a high chignon with a five-leave cap on it. The Buddha has a round face and partly bare upper body, holding a longevity bottle in his hands, sitting barefoot on the lotus throne, with necklaces, armlets, anklets, bracelets decorating his body.

Rhinoceros Horn Statue of the Cloth Bag Monk

Origin: Ming Dynasty

Height: 6 cm

Hammer Price: RMB 1,097,800

Name of Auction Company: Beijing Hanhai

Date of Transaction: 2001-07-02

This item carved out of a bright yellow rhino horn in full relief vividly describes the Cloth Bag Monk with big-long ears who puts his head and hands on his knees to take a break and enjoy the good time. The craftsman skillfully uses the brown tip of the horn to carve the head part, corresponding to the rosewood base, which brings about contrast of warm and cold colors.

Rhinoceros Horn Cup Carved with Pine, Bamboo and Plum Tree

Origin: Ming Dynasty

Height: 8 cm

Hammer Price: RMB 528,000

Name of Auction Company: Beijing Hanhai

Date of Transaction: 2004-11-22

This item is made of fine rhino horn, carved with pines, bamboos and plums, the three symbols of winter. It has an open mouth, a deep bottom, and a bamboo-shaped handle stretching from the bottom to the top. It is carved with a pine tree branch on the body, with a plum blossom on the top, accompanied by a flying bat. Superbly carved in high-relief and openwork, this item was a full representative of the taste of the literati of that time.

Rhinoceros Horn Cup Carved with Chinese Flowering Crabapple

Origin: Ming Dynasty

Length: 15 cm

Hammer Price: RMB 8,960,000

Name of Auction Company: Beijing Gutianyi

Date of Transaction: 2010-06-27

From the color, spots and texture, we can see this item is made of fine Sumatran rhino horn. It has shiny luster and a charming yellow color, with semi-transparent and smooth quality. It is decorated with a blossoming Chinese flowering crabapple which suits the refined and popular tastes, thus known as the Flower of the God, or the Princess Flower and the Noble Flower.

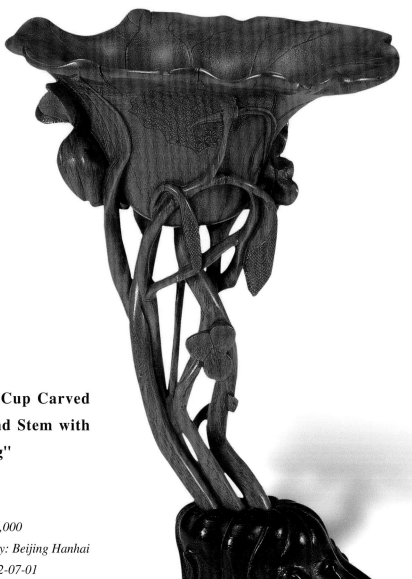

Rhinoceros Horn Cup Carved with Lotus leaf and Stem with Inscription "Bohong"

Origin: Ming Dynasty
Height: 21.5 cm
Hammer Price: RMB 132,000
Name of Auction Company: Beijing Hanhai
Date of Transaction: 2002-07-01

This item is an imitation of lotus leaf cup. It has an open mouth, shaped in lotus leaf. The body of the cup is carved with several interweaving lotus stems. It is put on a rosewood base. The whole item, using the relief carving and piercing, with elegant modeling, exquisite texture and smooth decoration lines, is really a masterpiece of rhino horn carving.

Rhinoceros Horn Cup Shaped in Chinese Flowering Crabapple with Two Dragon-shaped Handles

Origin: Ming Dynasty
Length: 20 cm
Hammer Price: RMB 11,405,600
Name of Auction Company: Hong Kong Sotheby' s
Date of Transaction: 2005-10-23

The body of this cup is shaped as Chinese Flowering Crabapple. It has an open mouth, a curving edge and a short foot. The cup handles are carved into two childlike like hornless dragons, each with a long curving tail, sharp claws holding on the cup edge and a stretched head looking inside the cup. With the novel design, lustrous material, natural texture, exquisite polishing, standardized craftsmanship, at the autumn auction of Hong Kong Sotheby' s, this item was sold at the record high price of Chinese cultural antiques in 2005.

Rhinoceros Horn Jue Cup with Taotie and Dragon Patterns

Origin: Ming Dynasty

Width: 19.6 cm   Height: 12.5 cm

Hammer Price: RMB 682,000

Name of Auction Company: Shanghai Jinghua

Date of Transaction: 2002-06-23

This item is an imitation product of bronze jue. It has a comparatively big body, a open mouth and a round foot, with fret patterns on the mouth and foot edges. It is decorated with a circle of taotie pattern on the body, relief carved with four hornless dragons on the handle, with three of them crawling on the cup mouth. It is also carved with other two vivid dragons on the flow part.

Rhinoceros Horn Cup Carved with a Hermit under the Pine Tree

Origin: Ming Dynasty
Height: 12.8cm
Hammer Price: RMB 454,500
Name of Auction Company: Beijing Hanhai
Date of Transaction: 1995-10-07

This cup is made of Asian rhinoceros horn. The carver uses relief carving and piercing to carve the handle part into a pine stem to connect the mouth and the foot of the cup. The body part is carved into a high mountain with green forest which is the place for the hermit to enjoy his life. It is really a masterpiece with lustrous color, elegant modeling and exquisite craftsmanship.

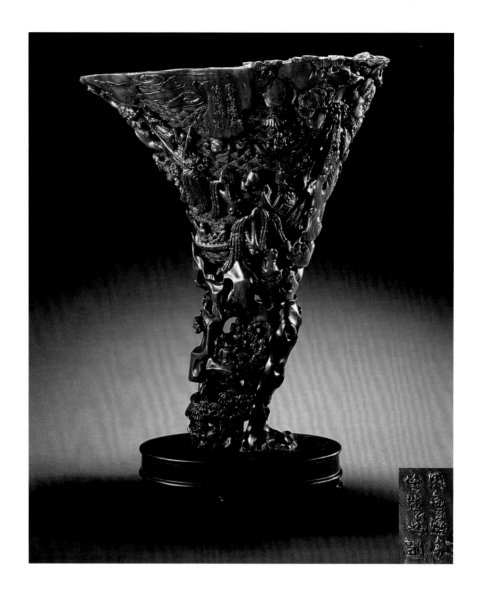

Rhinoceros Horn Cup Carved with "Fishing on the Autumn River" by Fang Hongzhai

Origin: Ming Dynasty
Height: 22.5 cm   Diameter: 17.5cm
Hammer Price: RMB 4,368,000   Name of Auction Company: Beijing Poly
Date of Transaction: 2008-12-06

This cup is made of a whole Indian rhino horn. With meticulous composition, the carver uses several techniques such as relief carving, circular carving and piercing to make it as a three-dimensional landscape painting. The upper part describes the fishing scene on the autumn river. The lower part describes the mountain stones and trees, with some peaceful scenes such as fishermen gathering for food, gentlemen walking, mothers feeding milk to children, which are a contrast to the active upper part.

Rhinoceros Horn Wine Cup without Holder

Origin: Late Ming Dynasty

Height: 13.2 cm

Hammer Price: RMB 6,549,880

Name of Auction Company: Hong Kong Christie' s

Date of Transaction: 2010-05-31

This cup is made of a Asian rhino horn which cuts the hollow out of the horn according to its shape. It has an open mouth and a tapered body. On the body it has two inscriptions, one is "the Reign of Emperor Wanli of the Ming Dynasty", the other is "the Treasure of the King of Ruichang". This kind of wine cup is without a holder, so when you give a toast, you must drink the whole cup of wine at one gulp.

Rhinoceros Horn Cup Carved with the Scene of "Lantingxu"

Origin: Late Ming Dynasty
Width: 16.6 cm
Hammer Price: RMB 34,997,080
Name of Auction Company: Hong Kong Christie' s
Date of Transaction: 2010-05-31

This cup is made of a giant Indian rhino horn which inscribes the scene of a banquet gathering of Wang Xizhi and others in the Orchid Pavilion, Shanyin County, in the Eastern Jin Dynasty. It is carved with eight human figures, with someone playing the stringed instrument, someone reading the poems and others drinking by the streams. Beside the people, it is carved with trees and bamboo forest. It has an inscription"Wu Heng"at the bottom.

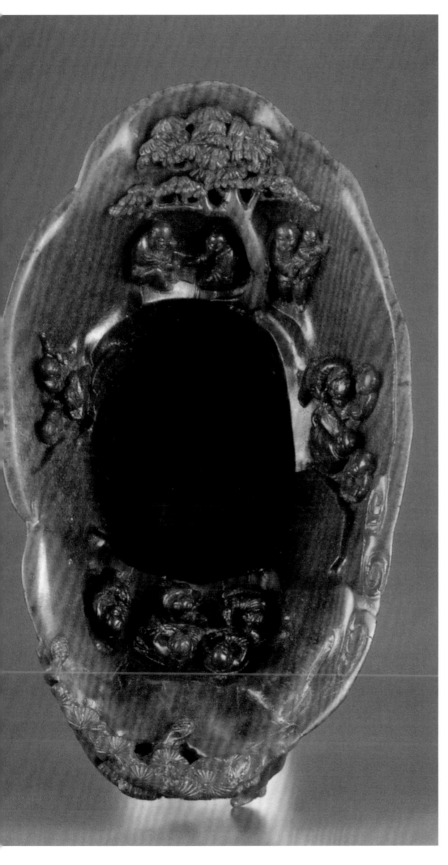

Rhinoceros Horn Cup Carved with One Hundred Children

Origin: Late Ming and Early Qing Dynasties
Height: 17.8 cm
Hammer Price:
RMB 22,213,400
Name of Auction
Company: Hong Kong
Christie's
Date of Transaction:
2010-05-31

The outer wall of this cup is carved with 64 children playing in the mountain forest with a stem of a pine tree as the handle. On the mouth part, it is carved with 16 children. It is also carved with bridges over streams, pavilions in the mountain. Every child has different appearances and is engaged in different games. The entire layout is full and well-arranged with distint gradations, which makes this item a masterpiece of the rhino horn craftsmanship.

Rhinoceros Horn Cup Carved into One Lotus with Inscription "Zhisheng"

Origin: Late Ming and Early Qing Dynasties

Height: 17.5 cm   Weight:274.5g

Hammer Price: RMB 7,187,400

Name of Auction Company: Hong Kong Christie's

Date of Transaction: 2008-05-27

This item is made of a whole rhino horn, carved into a lotus flower. It is hollow from the mouth to the bottom. The stem part is not attached to the body, but made of the same horn which is softened and curved by the steam. It has a seal character inscription"Zhisheng", which suggests it was made by a famous sculptor You Kan in the late Ming and early Qing Dynasties. He was famous as the craftsman of rhino horn carving, and later was recruited to the royal workshop. The lotus layout also has the meaning of consecutive successes in the Imperial Examination.

Rhinoceros Horn Cup Carved with Landscape and Human Figures with Inscription "Yeting"

Origin: Early Qing Dynasty
Length: 17.5 cm
Hammer Price: RMB 7,840,000
Name of Auction Company: Beijing Gutianyi
Date of Transaction: 2010-06-27

This cup is made of Asian rhino horn, with a comparatively big body and beeswax color. The outer wall is carved with mountain and water with pine trees. The main scene carved on the cup is an old man with long beards, wearing an official robe, putting some incense into a censer, with an absent-minded boy standing beside. The inscription "Yeting" was not found on previous records.

Rhinoceros Horn Cup Carved with Eight Horses of King Mu

Origin: Reign of Emperor Kangxi of Qing Dynasty

Height: 12.7 cm

Hammer Price: RMB 23,196,760

Name of Auction Company: Hong Kong Christie's

Date of Transaction: 2010-05-31

This item has an open mouth, a downward contracted belly and a flat bottom. The outer wall is carved with streams and maple trees. A maple tree stem is carved as the handle on one side which stretches inside to the mouth. Eight horses have different postures. Some of them are standing or lying, while the others are nestling up to each other. The two wranglers are enjoying their time under the tree beside the stream. It has an inscription of "the Eight Horses of King Mu". Another inscription is the name of Hanqing. The eight horses are the horses which are ridden by King Mu when he travels to the west land of Kunlun in the legend story. In ancient China, the fine horses are the symbol of the social status and the military power of the owner which are frequently used as the content of art.

Rhinoceros Horn Cup Carved with the Scene of "Night Cruise at the Red Cliff"

Origin: Reign of Emperor Kangxi of Qing Dynasty

Length: 16.5 cm   Weight: 323g

Hammer Price: RMB 1,500,800

Name of Auction Company: Beijing Poly   Date of Transaction: 2008-05-31

This cup is made of fine Asian rhino horn. It colors in dark red with the thin part a bit nonopaque. It has an open mouth, a downward contracted belly. The main scene carved on it is "Night Cruise at the Red Cliff". It uses the main part of the cup as the steep cliff with two pine trees stretching out and the stem used as the cup handle. In the curve of the river, a small boat is floating down, with Su Shi and two of his friends are chatting, the servant boy is cooking the tea and another person is holding oars on the stern. It has clear layout and fine arrangement.

Rhinoceros Horn Laifu Zun

Origin: Reign of Emperor Kangxi of Qing Dynasty
Height: 15.5 cm
Hammer Price: RMB 1,265,000
Name of Auction Company: Shanghai Jinghua
Date of Transaction: 2002-12-01

This item is made of a whole Indian rhino horn with an open mouth, a long neck, plump shoulders, a downward shrunk abdomen and a round foot. The body part is plain with no decoration. On the bottom it has an inscription "Made in the Royal Workshop in the Reign of Emperor Kangxi" with a red wood base which suggests that this item is a water bottle of the emperor himself. Laifu Zun is also called radish bottle which is a new product in the Reign of Emperor Kangxi. It has an auspicious meaning which means luck is coming.

Rhinoceros Horn Three-legged Jue Made by Royal Workshop

Origin: Reign of Emperor Kangxi of the Qing Dynasty

Height: 17 cm

Hammer Price: RMB 5,600,000

Name of Auction Company: Beijing Council

Date of Transaction: 2010-06-06

This cup has light brown color, which is an imitation product of the ancient bronze Jue. The craftsman cuts the sharp end of the rhino horn, removes something, and then heats the left part to make it look like three elephant teeth. The mouth is shaped like a long oval with two upward ends. On the body part near the mouth, it is carved with four different sized Chi dragons, which has the meaning of the old dragon teaching the young ones.

Rhinoceros Horn Carving of Zhang Qian in the Boat

Origin: Early Qing Dynasty
Length: 21cm
Hammer Price: RMB 8,960,000
Name of Auction Company: Beijing Poly
Date of Transaction: 2010-12-05

Compared with other ordinary shaped rhino horn items, the boat-shaped horn carving is an outstanding one which was cherished by emperors of Ming and Qing Dynasties. For Emperor Qianlong, he kept two boat-shaped rhino horn carving items now collected by Beijing Palace Museum and Taipei National Palace Museum separately. The content of the item is a legendary story about Zhang Qian taking a boat traveling in the heaven. The item colors in honey wax, carved according to the natural shape, with well-arranged layout. If you pour wine into the boat, you can drink it from the boat head.

Rhinoceros Horn Cup Carved with Flowers and Pheasants and Inscriptions of "Zhisheng"and "You kan"

Origin: Early Qing Dynasty
Height: 9.5cm
Hammer Price: RMB 2,464,000
Name of Auction Company: Beijing Hanhai
Date of Transaction: 2009-11-11

The main part of this cup is carved into a mountain rock, with a blossomy flower branch growing around it as the stem is carved as the cup handle. One pheasant crouches in the bush and the other one stands on the rock, which has the meaning of good luck. From the two inscriptions "Zhisheng" and "You kan", we know it is a product made by the famous horn carving master You kan.

Rhinoceros Horn Flower-shaped Gu Carved with Taotie Patterns

Origin: Reign of Emperor Qianlong of Qing Dynasty
Height: 25.1cm
Hammer Price:RMB 1,038,800
Name of Auction Company: Christie's
Date of Transaction: 2000-10-31

Gu is a bronze ritual goblet used in ancient time. This one is an imitation product made of rhino horn which is shaped as a Chinese flowering crabapple. It is tall and slender, with a slightly flared base that tapers to a slim center section before widening again into a trumpet-like mouth wider than the base. Its surface is decorated with taodie patterns.

Rhinoceros Horn Statue of Guanyin

Origin: Qing Dynasty
Height: 28 cm
Hammer Price: RMB 407,000
Name of Auction Company:
Beijing Hanhai
Date of Transaction: 2001-12-10

This item is a standing Guanyin statue carved out of rhino horn. With a high chignon on her head and eyes looking down, all the people are under her benevolent gaze. A vase in her left hand has water flowing down to the ground to make the wave which she is traveling on. With the elegant appearance, the statue has high artistic appeal.

Rhinoceros Horn Wenshu Statue of Manjusri

Origin: Qing Dynasty
Height: 19 cm
Hammer Price: RMB 1,064,000
Name of Auction Company: China Guardian
Date of Transaction: 2010-12-18

This Manjusri statue is carved out of a big smooth rhino horn. The Bodhisattva has a coronet on his chignon, a round elegant face, a bare upper body covered with necklaces and wreaths. He is riding on a lion which is set on a lotus base. Manjusri Bodhisattva is one of the top four Bodhisattvas in Buddhism who is famous for his wisdom.

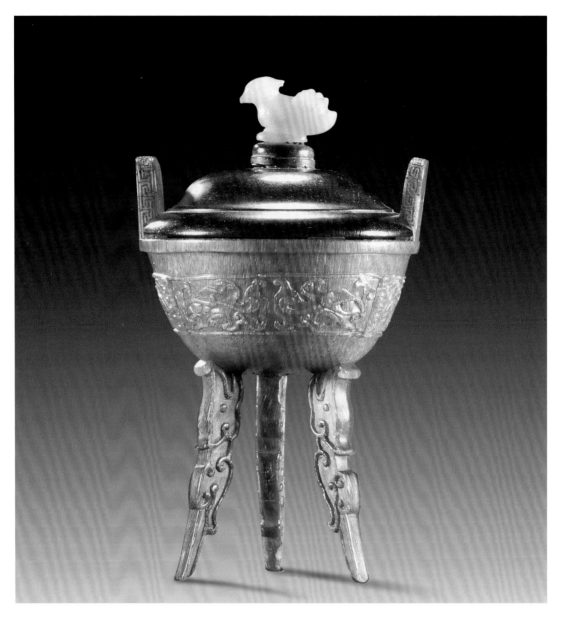

Rhinoceros Horn Tripod with Taotie and Dragon Patterns

Origin: Qing Dynasty

Diameter: 8.7 cm

Hammer Price: RMB 3,688,800

Name of Auction Company: Hong Kong Sotheby's

Date of Transaction: 2005-10-23

This tripod is carved out of a whole rhino horn. It colors as the candied date. The layout is an imitation of the bronze ding. It has two upward ears, a round belly and three standing feet. The belly part is relief carved with taotie pattern. The feet are decorated with dragon patterns. It also has a rosewood cover with a bird-shaped white jade knob.

Rhinoceros Horn Kettle

Origin: Qing Dynasty
Height: 24.8 cm
Hammer Price: RMB 1,600,000
Name of Auction Company: Hong Kong Christie's
Date of Transaction: 2001-10-16

This kettle is made of Asian Rhino horn. Its cover looks like a helmet with dark color and a lion knob. On one side is a long spout without decorative pattern; on the other side is the handle which is shaped like a dragon. From the bottom to the top, the body part is relief carved with four different layers of decorative patterns which makes it become a masterpiece of horn carving products.

Rhinoceros Horn Cup Carved with Grapes and Squirrels (one pair)

Origin: Qing Dynasty

Height: 40 cm

Hammer Price: RMB 1,595,000

Name of Auction Company: Liaoning Internatinal

Date of Transaction: 2006-06-17

This pair of cups are carved out of rhino horn according to its nature shape. It has a big body, smooth light dark color. It is carved with grape vines as the cup body with its mouth open as a flower. The body is decorated with grapes and vines with six squirrels playing inside. Several flower branches become the base of the cup. The grapes and squirrels have the symbolic meaning of increasing fertility.